T0065266

STORIES UNTOLD

A History and Genealogical Study of the Mays,
Bellamy, Parkhill, and Other Related Families

LAURA MAYS

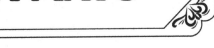

STORIES UNTOLD
A HISTORY AND GENEALOGICAL STUDY OF THE MAYS, BELLAMY, PARKHILL, AND OTHER RELATED FAMILIES

Copyright © 2021 Laura Mays.

All rights reserved. No part of this book may be used or reproduced by any means, graphic, electronic, or mechanical, including photocopying, recording, taping or by any information storage retrieval system without the written permission of the author except in the case of brief quotations embodied in critical articles and reviews.

iUniverse books may be ordered through booksellers or by contacting:

iUniverse
1663 Liberty Drive
Bloomington, IN 47403
www.iuniverse.com
844-349-9409

Because of the dynamic nature of the Internet, any web addresses or links contained in this book may have changed since publication and may no longer be valid. The views expressed in this work are solely those of the author and do not necessarily reflect the views of the publisher, and the publisher hereby disclaims any responsibility for them.

Any people depicted in stock imagery provided by Getty Images are models, and such images are being used for illustrative purposes only. Certain stock imagery © Getty Images.

ISBN: 978-1-6632-2784-3 (sc)
ISBN: 978-1-6632-2841-3 (hc)
ISBN: 978-1-6632-2783-6 (e)

Library of Congress Control Number: 2021916929

Print information available on the last page.

iUniverse rev. date: 08/24/2021

PROLOGUE

I come from a long line of ancestors who have strived to preserve the past. My mother's family traces back to Italy and my father has direct roots to the *old south*. I am 22 years old and have lived in New Jersey with my family my entire life except for three and a half years in college at the University of Delaware. I am a creative, a writer, a cook, a baker, an artist, a historian—I am a lot of things.

Before I begin, it is important for my own moral compass as well as for readers to know that I am not writing about my ancestors in support of what they did or the specific ways they chose to live their lives. When studying history or even in trying to understand current events, people often view the past with a modern-day lens using present values to judge the social or economic conditions of the past. While history will hold historical figures accountable for any actions diverging from the cultural norms of their time, they still must be examined in accordance with those cultural norms. People cannot be properly understood unless their environments and the social constructs in which they lived are considered also. We must understand why people did what they did in order to learn from them.

We cannot go forward unless we understand what we have left behind. To quote philosopher George Santayana, "Those who cannot remember the past are condemned to repeat it."

With that, I could not agree more.

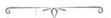

I began my research for this book long before I knew it would actually be published. I was twelve or thirteen years old when I discovered Ancestry.com. As a young child, I was captivated by history, always dragging my family to a museum on every vacation. My mom has even said that one of my first favorite toys as a child was a globe. I've always loved learning about the past and people's stories—especially my own.

Even at the ripe old age of thirteen, I was intrigued with solving the puzzle of my family's genealogy. I started with what I knew from my grandparents, used the Ancestry's records, and dug deeper and deeper into the past until I reached a point where I felt my findings may no longer be accurate. How can a person really know their exact lineage all the way back to 1050? So, I got to a point where I could not go back any further. I was happy partially because I felt a sense of accomplishment for doing the research, but also because I finally had something to talk to my grandfather about. He wrote a book several years prior about his life and family, and so I knew he was also interested in the subject. When we would go to their house in North Carolina over the summers, I would show him my research and he would smile back at me, and honestly, that was all the validation I needed. These activities might seem entirely odd for a young adolescent girl to be so interested in, but I loved every minute of it. I never considered myself to be like everyone else anyway.

Not too long after I reached a stopping point on Ancestry, my interest declined and I began to turn my attention towards other activities. I was in high school and still loved my history classes, and eventually decided that I would study history in college. Throughout the three and a half years, I learned so much fascinating information that has transformed me into an immensely better writer and storyteller.

Everything I have done in my life has led me right here. From writing short stories and novels and playing with maps and my presidents list placemat as a child, to earning my bachelor's degree in history as an adult; writing this book about my personal history and the people who I come from makes so much sense. I did not see it myself initially, but I'm so glad my grandfather did.

He is the one who asked me to write this book and encouraged me to tell these stories. He has guided me in every step along the way, and for that I am so grateful. I dedicate this book to him.

CHAPTER ONE

My Present

Most of my book was written in the year 2020. Now it is 2021, the year I will publish this book, and I am 22 years old. I grew up in the very normal middle-class suburban town of Freehold, New Jersey. It is a little over an hour from New York City, 30 minutes from the beach, although most people in New Jersey call it *the shore*, and we have all four seasons with snow days and blazing hot summers. Some may say it is the perfect place to live. I am not sure if it's entirely perfect, but it has been a wonderful place to grow up. My mom, my dad, and my sister are my immediate family. Both of my grandparents on my mother's side lived with us, however my grandma died in 2016 from Leukemia, leaving my grandpa who lives with us now. Fortunately, our house is large enough so that I've always been able to have my own room when I've wanted to. When I was a child, my sister and I decided to move all of our furniture into my room so that her room could be the designated "American Girl Doll Room." My parents gave us the freedom to express ourselves in a lot of ways, including by letting us give our dolls their own bedroom.

Growing up, my sister and I played competitive softball and my dad was always one of our coaches. For about ten years, my parents spent almost every weekend either watching or coaching softball. They would drive us to tournaments sometimes hours away, and then spend hours outside in the sun, rain, wind, and, even snow.

When it came time to make a decision for college, the University of Delaware was an easy choice. My oldest cousin on my mom's side, Christa Bramante, graduated four years prior to my entering so I already had visited the campus with her and knew I loved it. However, getting used to being away from home was a bit more complicated than I expected and I had some trouble making genuine friends in the beginning. It took time and it took putting myself out there for it to happen, but eventually it did happen. To make a friend you have to first be a friend. The University of Delaware was the best place that I could ever have attended. I met my closest friends, met my boyfriend of almost three years now, and learned so much, both about my major and about myself. I can honestly say that I am a very different person now than who I was upon entering college.

Since graduating in December of 2019, I did an internship at Weber Shandwick, a huge PR agency in New York City, and worked on its Anheuser Busch account, specifically on the Budweiser and Stella Artois Super Bowl XLIV campaigns. Budweiser's campaign was a TV spot titled *'Typical Americans,'* and Stella Artois' campaign was an event held in Miami near the stadium where the game was being played. That was another major learning experience!

I spent the first two weeks of March interviewing for full-time jobs, got a job, and was supposed to start on March 17, 2020. Then New York City was shut down on March 14. The COVID-19 pandemic finally reached the United States in its full force and hit New York after beginning in Seattle. My job was put on hold until further notice, possibly indefinitely, and the entire country shut down for quite some time. Initially, COVID-19 was at its worst in the tri-state area (New York, New Jersey, and Connecticut), so I was following especially strict rules. From March to May I did not leave the house except for walks or to the grocery store. I am thankful for that time because it granted me the opportunity to research and write this book—something I may never have had the time to do if I were working a full-time job and commuting four hours a day. In October, I was offered a full-time position at Weber Shandwick in the same department I initially interned in, and now, as I finish this book, I am also beginning my new career.

Beyond my immediate family, my father's siblings reside throughout the Eastern United States. My grandparents live in Florida, but have a second home in Highlands, North Carolina, and my aunts, uncles, and cousins live in Pinehurst and Wake Forest, North Carolina and Atlanta, Georgia. We are spread out, but all come together every couple of summers at either my grandparents' home in Highlands or at a beach house in Hilton Head, South Carolina. My dad and his three siblings grew up in Lakeland, Florida. They spent their summers in Highlands, but mainly grew up among the close-knit community in Lakeland. You can read more about this history in my grandfather's book, *Proud Heritage*. His book will provide a more detailed account, but I will give a brief background on my family as they are all essential parts to these stories.

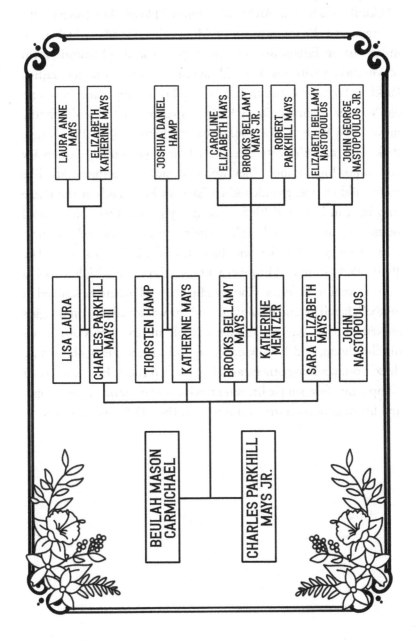

LAURA ANNE MAYS

ELIZABETH KATHERINE MAYS

JOSHUA DANIEL HAMP

CAROLINE ELIZABETH MAYS

BROOKS BELLAMY MAYS JR.

ROBERT PARKHILL MAYS

ELIZABETH BELLAMY NASTOPOULOS

JOHN GEORGE NASTOPOULOS JR.

LISA LAURA

CHARLES PARKHILL MAYS III

THORSTEN HAMP

KATHERINE MAYS

BROOKS BELLAMY MAYS

KATHERINE MENTZER

SARA ELIZABETH MAYS

JOHN NASTOPOULOS

BEULAH MASON CARMICHAEL

CHARLES PARKHILL MAYS JR.

5

On January 10, 1936, my grandfather, Charles Parkhill Mays Jr. (Parkhill), was born at Archbald Memorial Hospital in Thomasville, Georgia, just 20 miles north of Monticello, Florida, which is 26 miles east of Tallahassee. He grew up in the small historic town of Monticello with his sister, Elizabeth, mother, Katherine, father, Parkhill Sr., and grandmother, Emmala Bellamy Parkhill, in an old Victorian home built by his grandparents in 1885. The family moved to a farm at Miccosukee (near Monticello) in 1943 where Parkhill Jr. and Elizabeth attended a four-room country elementary and junior high school. They would spend the summers, just like their children and grandchildren later, in Highlands at the home they built in 1947 and 1948. During my grandfather's high school years, the family moved back to their home in Monticello to help care for his grandmother, who had suffered a bad stroke in the late 1940s. Parkhill Jr. and Elizabeth, known throughout high school as Maisie, went to Jefferson County High School, where he lettered in football, baseball, and basketball, and she was an all-star on the girls basketball team. My grandfather has told me so many stories from his childhood, and I really encourage all to read his book because these stories, among others, are also featured there. He truly gives a glimpse into how simple life was growing up on a farm and in a small and historic southern town throughout the 1930s, 40s, and 50s.

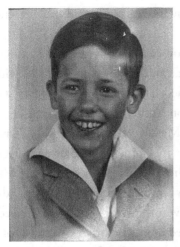

Charles Parkhill Mays Jr. as a child (left) and in
his 20s in the army at Fort Sill (right).

After graduating from high school, Elizabeth attended Randolph-Macon Women's College, renamed Randolph-Macon College, in Lynchburg, Virginia and eventually transferred to the University of Florida, where she would complete her degree in education. Later, she attended Katherine Gibbs, a well-known secretarial school in New York, and married George York Mills Jr. in 1957. George and Elizabeth had three children, Katherine Cornelia, York III, and Parkhill Scott. Cornelia graduated from Randolph-Macon as well and starred in its theater. She lives in New York City now, beginning her career in the theater and later becoming an executive assistant to corporate level officers. York attended Mercer University in Macon, Georgia and is married to Sandra Jane Dockery. They have two children, Alexandra Elizabeth and York IV. York is with HDR Engineering, Inc. serving as an embedded consultant in the Office of Right of Way at The Florida Development of Transportation. Scott graduated from Florida State University and Indiana University Kelley School of Business, and was married to Susan Tillotson. They had two sons, Austin Parkhill and Trevor Scott. Scott began his career with Ford Motor Company in Dearborn, a suburb of Detroit, and is currently with FedEx.

Parkhill attended Washington & Lee University in Lexington, Virginia, pledging Kappa Alpha and graduating in 1958 with a degree in economics. He attended law school at the University of Florida and graduated number one in his class in early 1961.

My grandmother, Beulah Mason Carmichael, was born on January 29, 1939 and grew up in Gainesville, Florida with her parents, Parks and Beulah, and her brother, John. Her father, Parks Carmichael, was a recognized lawyer throughout Gainesville and the State of Florida. He practiced law for 56 years and was involved in hundreds of cases, as well as served on the Board of Governors of the Florida Bar. He was born on April 2, 1909 in Monticello and lived in Drifton, a few miles south of Monticello, with his mother and sister until the eighth grade when he moved to Gainesville to live with his Aunt Lula and Uncle Sidney Robertson.[1] Parks' mother, Nellie Bird Carmichael, owned a dress shop in Monticello that she named "Milady's Shop." Prior to my grandparents ever meeting, Nellie had actually tried to set them up in Monticello over numerous summers. Mason graduated from Gainesville High School and attended the University of Florida.

A young Mason Carmichael.

While in his first semester of law school, Parkhill was set up on a blind date and all he knew about his date was that she was a sophomore Chi Omega. That girl turned out to be my grandmother, Mason Carmichael, and from then on, they dated continuously throughout their years at the University of Florida (she finished undergrad in three years and he finished law school in two and a half). Only a few days after their graduations, they were married at the First Presbyterian Church in Gainesville. Parkhill passed the bar exam that April and he and Mason headed off to the army at Fort Sill, Oklahoma, with his final duty station at Fort Rucker, Alabama until his discharge in late December, 1963. He and Mason moved to Tampa, Florida where he would begin his first position as a practicing attorney, and she would continue teaching for a short time.

My grandparents moved from Tampa to Lakeland in September

of 1964 upon realizing that the city life was just not for two people who grew up on a farm and in small towns. They rented a small house before purchasing the home that they still live in on Cambridge Avenue overlooking Lake Hollingsworth. Although there have been many additions over the years, from what I understand, the original house is still the same as it was when Parkhill and Mason moved in, in 1964, and the same as when my father, Charles Parkhill III, was born in 1965. A little over a year later, my father's sister, Katherine Mason Mays, or Aunt Sissy as I know her, was born. In 1971, my Uncle Brooks (Brooks Bellamy Mays) was born, and then finally, in 1974, my Aunt Sara (Sara Elizabeth Mays) was born. Their family, as well as the house, grew simultaneously as my grandfather's law practice did also. He is a 60-year member of the Florida Bar, and juggled work and family with my grandmother who was an active member of the Lakeland community as well as a devoted mother.

My father attended Washington and Lee University, following in his father's and his great-grandfather's footsteps, before marrying my mother, Lisa Laura (her maiden name is the origin of my first name). My mom was born and raised in Brooklyn, New York, just as her parents were, and attended St. Francis College in Brooklyn. Her great-grandparents immigrated to the United States from Italy in the late 1800s and early 1900s settling into the Italian immigrant communities throughout Manhattan and Brooklyn.

My parents met while working together at Arthur Anderson, a large accounting firm in New York. Upon marrying in 1990, they moved into an apartment in Battery Park City in downtown Manhattan, overlooking the harbor and the Statue of Liberty. My mother later joined Goldman Sachs and my father turned his attention to business. After several other business ventures, he later became a founder and the President of a tech company, STOPit Solutions. In 1993 they moved across the river to Edgewater, New Jersey, where both Elizabeth and I were born. Our first home was a condominium in the gated community of Independence Harbor (for the longest time as a child, I thought that it was "Independent

Harbor") which overlooked the Hudson River. Our second home (where we lived while our current house was being built) was an apartment also overlooking the river. I remember nights spent by the window with my baby sister looking out to see what colors the Empire State Building would be shining. When I was in kindergarten we moved to our newly built home on Equinox Lane in Freehold, New Jersey, where we have been ever since. As I said, I am 22 now and Elizabeth is 19 and a freshman at the University of South Carolina. Interestingly, I came across a document originally printed in the South Carolina Magazine of Ancestral Research that credited a direct ancestor, Samuel Mays, as one of the University founders.[2]

Aunt Sissy attended Boston University, and following in the footsteps of her mother and grandmother, Katherine Bell Mays, began teaching in Central Florida after graduation. She then married Thorsten Hamp, a software engineer, who had immigrated to the United States from Germany. They lived in Orlando and later moved to Wake Forest, North Carolina. In 2004, while still in Orlando they welcomed a new addition to their family: my cousin Josh. They recently built a new home (in 2020) in Youngsville, North Carolina, on the outskirts of Wake Forest.

Uncle Brooks graduated from Furman University before attending the University of South Carolina College of Medicine and went on to become a doctor at Pinehurst Medical Clinic. While in medical school, he married Kathryn Mentzer, and they have since had my cousins: Caroline, born in 2001, Brooks Jr., born in 2003, and Robbie, born in 2005. Caroline is only a few weeks younger than Elizabeth and is a freshman at the University of North Carolina.

Aunt Sara also attended Furman University, and following graduation became a CPA. After 6 years with Arthur Anderson as a manager, she assisted in the closing of the Atlanta office. She then joined Ernst & Young, where she is now a Managing Director. She married John Nastopoulos, a second-generation Greek American (and an E&Y Partner), and they had my cousins Elizabeth, whom we call Lily, in 2007, and John Jr., who we call J.J., in 2010. In

2006, Aunt Sara and Uncle John were asked to relocate temporarily to Ernst & Young's national office in Cleveland, but moved back to Atlanta before J.J. was born.

My grandfather likes to call us an "International Family" and I couldn't agree more. I find it extremely "American" how one family line that traces back to the earliest settlers of the United States melded with three, very distinct, European cultures: my mom's Italian heritage, my Uncle Thorsten's German heritage, and my Uncle John's Greek heritage.

Beyond my family members who are still living, I will separate each chapter by significant family lines. There are many last names and several lines that split up and branch off so I am also providing images of the physical family trees throughout to make it as simple as possible to follow.

CHAPTER TWO

The Mays Family

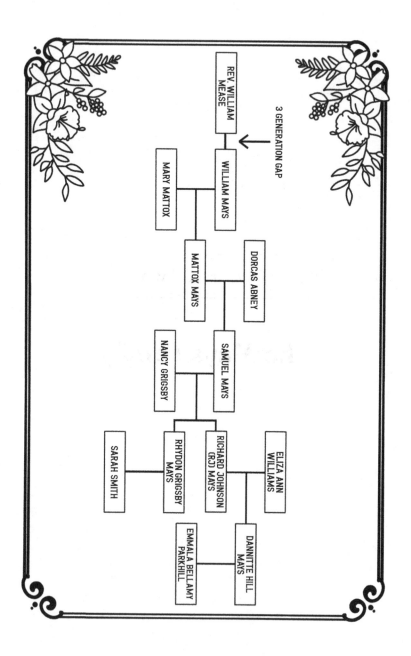

3 GENERATION GAP

REV. WILLIAM MEASE

WILLIAM MAYS — MARY MATTOX

MATTOX MAYS — DORCAS ABNEY

SAMUEL MAYS — NANCY GRIGSBY

RICHARD JOHNSON (RJ) MAYS — RHYDON GRIGSBY MAYS — SARAH SMITH

ELIZA ANN WILLIAMS

DANNITTE HILL MAYS — EMMALA BELLAMY PARKHILL

14

The history of the Mays family in the United States is extensive and has endured since even before the founding of the United States. The story most likely began with Reverend William Mease, who immigrated to Jamestown from England in 1611 with 300 other settlers. There are two origin stories for the family name, "Mease" (also spelled "Maise" or "Mase," and many other ways). The first is that the family is Norman and the name was originally found in a town called Massey in Normandy, France. Most of the town residents adopted a similar surname which was later brought to England by the Norman invasion. For context, the Normans, led by William, Duke of Normandy, invaded England in 1066. The invasion brought new people and a new culture to certain regions that were formerly solely Anglo Saxon, until eventually things just blended to create the English culture.

The second origin story, stated by another Samuel Mays in his book, *Genealogy of The Mays Family and Related Families*, says that "Mays" or "Mease" is the modern form of the name "Maas." There was a family in Holland that traces back to 1476 with the name "Maas," after the River Meuse (Maas in Dutch) and the city of Maastricht, where the family lived. In 1871, there was also correspondence with Rev. John Mase, a Wesleyan minister in Belfast, Ireland, in which he revealed that his family descended from three Dutch brothers who came to Belfast with William of Orange from Holland in 1688. The rationale behind this theory is that if Dutch Maas descendants could immigrate to Ireland, they could also have immigrated to England.[3]

Regardless of which story is true, the name "Mease," or other related spellings, began to appear in England in the late 11th and 12th centuries. Written records were not widespread in England that long ago, thus names were often spelled phonetically. The earliest records of Maes, Mease, Mays, and Mayse are found in old parish registers in London.[4]

Reverend William Mease was mentioned in many letters and documents and there is proof that he did live in both England

and the United States, but the connection between my ancestors and him is unclear. It is not uncommon for there to be a lack of clarity as genealogy dates back so far. Although there is much research connecting William Mease to the modern-day American Mays family, no sources contain complete confirmation. Early on as a history major, I learned that there are always mistakes, even in information deemed factual. History is studied continuously because researchers are constantly learning new things and uncovering more details from the past. This constant analysis allows historians to amend and correct previous errors, making records and information as accurate as possible.

William Mease came to the *new world* as a 37 years old minister and established a church at the settlement in Jamestown. There is a church in Hampton, Virginia named St. John's that is supposedly near the sight of the original church where William ministered. A sign at the church reads:

> Near here on the church creek stood the first church
> at Kecoughtan [later Hampton], built on the parish
> Glebe Farm about 1616, as the first church of the
> oldest continuous settlement of English origin
> in America. William Mease was the first known
> minister of the parish, from 1613 until about 1620.[5]

In 1623, following the Great Massacre of 1622 by Native Americans, William, among other prominent colonists, returned to England to shed light on life in the colony. There are also letters from John Rolf to King James I of England describing conditions of the colony that include mention of William Mease. The date of his return to Virginia and his death are unknown, but genealogical records of the early Virginian families show that he purchased land along the Appomattox River and that he had two sons, Henry and John.[6] St. John's Church features a reproduction of the seal of the society that originally sent William and other missionaries to America.

I have been able to accurately trace the Mays family line back to my great great great great great great grandfather, William Mays. Virginia genealogical records connect William Mays to William Mease through one of William Mease's sons. The records of the sons, John and Henry, are ambiguous so there is uncertainty as to exactly who the sons married and which children belonged to which son.[7] Based on these genealogical records, my judgement is that William Mays, my six times great grandfather, and his son, Mattox Mays, my five times great grandfather, are descendants of Rev. William Mease. A common problem in genealogy is that oftentimes people name their children after another relative, causing everyone to share very similar names. Unfortunately, I ran into this issue repeatedly.

William Mays was born in Nottoway, Virginia in 1680 and married Mary Mattox on March 9, 1713. Their son was Mattox Mays, named after his mother, who was born in 1730 in Halifax, Virginia and died in 1773. Mattox was married to Dorcas Abney, with whom he had many children including Samuel Mays, my great great great great grandfather. In his will, Mattox left Dorcas his entire estate and stated that he was entrusting his good friend, William Hill, to assist his wife in selling the family land to purchase more *appropriate* land for a woman.[8] Mattox wanted his wife to be able to sustain herself without having the burden of an extensive plot of land. After William helped Dorcas sell the old land and purchase a new plot with the money earned, they began a romantic relationship which led to marriage. William and Dorcas had one son named Dennett Hill. When Dorcas finally passed away in 1804, she stated in her will that the entirety of her estate be left to her second husband, William Hill, and their son, Dennett Hill. Only if Dennett died without heirs would the property ever descend to her Mays children.[9] Essentially, all of Mattox Mays and Dorcas Abney's children were excluded from receiving any family money and cut completely out of the family estate upon their mother's death. Dorcas left everything to her second family. Odd enough, despite Dennett Hill inheriting Mattox Mays' entire monetary estate at the expense of Mattox's own children, the name Dennett Hill (eventually spelled "Dannitte Hill") is actually quite popular in the Mays family even to this day. The frequency in which this name appears will become more apparent as the chapter goes on.

Samuel Mays, one of the children of Mattox and Dorcas, was born on July 23, 1762 in Halifax, Virginia. According to "Virginia Historical Genealogies," by John Bennett Boddie, Samuel Mays was in three battles of the Revolutionary War before he was 16 years old: The Battle of Musgrove Mills, Blackstocks, and Hanging Rocks in General Sumter's Brigade.[10] He was a member of the legislature in Newberry County, South Carolina and a Brigadier General during the War of 1812. Despite being removed from his father's will, he and his wife, Nancy, were extremely wealthy, owning thousands of acres of land in South Carolina, and he was one of the alleged founders of the University of South Carolina.[11]

Nancy was born on March 12, 1775 to Enoch Grigsby and

Mary Susan "Mollie" Butler—both of prominent families in Edgefield, South Carolina. Enoch was a doctor and a lieutenant in the Revolutionary War, and he and Mollie lived on a plantation near Mount Willing. Mollie Butler was an aunt to the eminent General William Butler, as well as an aunt to Elizabeth Butler, mother of Behethland Brooks Simkins Bird (my great great great great great grandmother). More about Behethland and the Brooks family later.

Returning to the Mays family line, Samuel Mays and Nancy Grigsby had 10 children, the seventh of whom was Richard Johnson Mays, born January 8, 1808. Richard Johnson, or R.J., married Eliza Ann Williams, whose grandfather, James Williams, was born in England and served as a captain in the Virginia Continental Line in the Revolution.[12] R.J. and Eliza were married in 1830 when he was 21 and she was only 14. They moved from South Carolina to Florida in 1831 and settled along Bellamy Road near Lake Sampala in Madison County to be near R.J.'s older brother, Rhyden Grigsby Mays, who had already moved to Florida.[13] In 1833, R.J. and Eliza moved to the northern part of the county where they would build Clifton Mansion on their plantation (12 miles west of Madison, 12 miles south of Quitman, GA, and 18 miles east of Monticello), expanding the family's reach as wealthy planters throughout Florida. Beyond farming, R.J. was also heavily involved in the social and political affairs of the community and even the state. He established "Mays Academy" on their plantation to provide an education for his eleven children as well as neighbors in and around Madison County. From 1835 to 1838, R.J. was the postmaster in Madison County and in 1837, was named Justice of the Peace. In 1845, representing the planter class, he was a delegate to the constitutional convention that met in St. Joseph to frame the first constitution of the State of Florida.[14]

Portraits of R.J. Mays (left) and Eliza Ann Williams (right).

R.J. was a renowned religious and cultural leader as well, serving as clerk of the Hickstown Church, the precursor to the First Baptist Church of Madison. He also assisted in organizing the Elizabeth Baptist Church near Monticello and the Concord Baptist Church in the northern county, where he served as the pastor for a time. From 1840 to 1860, R.J. helped establish the Monticello Baptist Church, the Liberty Baptist Church in Brooks County, Georgia, and the Piney Grove Baptist Church. Arguably his greatest accomplishment, R.J. was known as the "Father of the Florida Baptist Convention," first officially held on Monday, November 20th, 1854 at 8 P.M. in the parlor of Clifton Mansion. The gathering was composed of 17 delegates from the three other Baptist organizations in Florida at the time, and R.J. was elected as the first convention president. The delegates met around a stunning round dining table that is still in my family today. In a letter to Linda Demott dated March 16, 2000, my grandfather described the table that is sitting in my grandparents' home in Lakeland:

> The marble top table which measures 6 feet 2 inches
> across and weighs about 1,000 pounds and around

which the Baptist Association [Convention] of Florida was formed, is now in my breakfast room in Lakeland.... This table, which was brought to Madison County in the 1820s or 1830s from New York via St. Marks was moved from Madison County, probably in the late 1800s, to Greenville, South Carolina, [for R.J. and Eliza's daughter], Mary Mays, who married Fox Beatty. The marble top table stayed in the old Beatty house in Greenville until about 1948, when the Beatty family passed away and the old home in the middle of Greenville, South Carolina, was relocated to the outskirts and became a home for the Garden Center. My father went to Greenville with a farm trailer and moved the table back to Miccosukee where we then lived and where it stayed until about 1954 when my parents moved back to the old house in Monticello that was built by D. H. [Dannitte Hill] Mays, son of R. J. Mays, in 1885. My parents stayed in that house until about [1978] when the house burned all around the table, but left it standing and unhurt. I went up and moved the table down to Lakeland in about [1978 or 1979], where it has been since that time.[15]

On April 8, 1852, R.J. and Eliza's youngest son, Dannitte Hill Mays, was born on the plantation at Clifton Mansion. His name was derived from an immigrant ancestor of Virginia, Dennett Abney, father of Dorcas Abney who was wife to Mattox Mays. The name was given to many of Abney's descendants, including the son of Dorcas Abney and her second husband, William Hill. As previously said, their son Dennett Hill was Dannitte Hill Mays' namesake.

Growing up, R.J. and Eliza's son, Dannitte, attended public schools in Savannah, Georgia and was a student at Washington &

Lee from 1866 to 1869 when General Robert E. Lee was President of the university. Dannitte did not have the money to graduate because his family was left in an arduous financial situation after the Civil War. The family plantation was mortgaged to afford supplies for the Confederate army and on July 18th, 1864, R.J. died at Clifton Mansion. After leaving Washington & Lee in 1869, Dannitte began to supervise for other planters throughout the region and acquire properties in Jefferson, Madison, and Leon counties—7,000 acres and farms all operated by tenants.[16] He was also a deacon in the Methodist Episcopal Church for over 15 years, and an avid hunter and fisherman.

Prior to R.J.'s death, Eliza assisted him in affairs both in and out of the home and ran the plantation when he was overcome by illness. She lived at Clifton Mansion for 18 years after R.J.'s death, moving in with her daughter Mary in 1883 in Greenville, South Carolina. Eliza survived her husband by 26 years, passing away in 1890.[17]

On June 2, 1880 at Monticello, Dannitte Hill Mays married Emmala Bellamy Parkhill, daughter of George Washington Parkhill and Elizabeth Brooks Bellamy, both from prestigious families throughout Florida and Edgefield, South Carolina. I will further discuss the Parkhill, Bellamy, and Brooks families in chapters to come. Emmala and Dannitte had six children: Elizabeth Parkhill (Lizzie), Mary Eliza (Mamie), Emmala Parkhill, Sara Croom, Dannitte Hill Jr., and Charles Parkhill, who my lineage runs through. I will outline the progeny of each child of Dannitte and Emmala at the end of this chapter in addition to tracing those of Charles Parkhill.

In 1885, Dannitte built a large Victorian home in the northwestern part of Monticello. My grandfather, Parkhill Jr., grew up in this home with his father, mother, sister, and grandmother, Emmala Bellamy Parkhill. It was also the home that burned in a fire on July 12th, 1978. My grandfather recalls stories that his grandmother, Emmala, told him about how proud she was of Dannitte for being an excellent quail hunter. It brought her so much joy every time he would bring quail home in his hunting bags that were opened and poured onto a sheet for the quail to be cleaned.

Dannitte and Emmala's home in Monticello
(left) and a portrait of Dannitte (right).

After establishing a livery stable, cotton gin, and other means of support, Dannitte turned to a distinguished political career in 1888 as a delegate from Jefferson County to the Florida Democratic State Convention. By 1890, he was elected as Jefferson County's representative to the Florida State Legislature, serving on the committees on Rules and State Institutions from 1891 to 1893, and on the committees on Finance and Taxation, Public Health, Public Printing, Appropriations, and Railroads and Telegraphs from 1895 to 1897, in addition to being Speaker of the House.[18] In both 1900 and 1904, Dannitte lost the Florida gubernatorial nominations by just several votes first to William Sherman Jennings and second to Napoleon Bonaparte Broward.[19] Both would later become Florida Governors. In 1908, Dannitte announced his candidacy for the United States House of Representatives for Florida's third congressional district running as a Democrat.[20] His platform had four essential components: Dannitte would improve Florida waterway systems to meet the demands of the state's growing commercialization, enhance rural free delivery systems, attain government aid to build new roads, and back state labor unions. In the April 16, 1908 edition of the *Madison's New Enterprise* newspaper, Dannitte stated:

> As a Floridian born and bred, I invite and solicit my people's support. Having been a farmer always, I may have missed some of the strenuous features of modern life; but I claim that this will not alienate from me, a filler of the soil, the support of the people, nor disqualify me from serving them faithfully as a congressman.[21]

He won the nomination even against the five other democrats and faced Republican William H. Northup in the election. Dannitte prevailed once again in the general election and served in the House of Representatives from 1908 to 1910, and then again from 1910 to 1912.[22] After a long career in politics and running the family plantations, Dannitte Hill Mays died in Monticello on May 9th, 1930, leaving the old Mays homestead to his wife and children. Dannitte had previously given to each of his children 1,600 acres, more or less, of land in Jefferson County.

The youngest son of Dannitte and Emmala, Charles Parkhill Mays, was born on June 20, 1902. He was named after Emmala's brother, Charles Breckenridge Parkhill. Charles Breckenridge Parkhill became a prosecutor in Escambia County, Florida, served as Florida Supreme Court Justice, and married Genevieve Perry, daughter of former Florida governor, Edward A. Perry. I will discuss more about the Parkhill family, as well as other related families in the chapters to come.

As previously said, Charles Parkhill, who went by "Parkhill," grew up in Monticello with his siblings and parents and attended the University of Florida pledging Kappa Alpha. Parkhill's accomplishments were well dealt with by his ever-respectful son and my grandfather in his book, *Proud Heritage*. Suffice it to say that he followed in his father, Dannitte's, footsteps with a career in agriculture managing Tuscawilla Plantation along with the Jefferson County plantations, and in politics as a County Commissioner and state legislator. When Parkhill was 27, he met 16-year-old Claudia Katherine Bell (Katherine), who was a student at Monticello High School and from Coalfire and Andalusia, Alabama. Katherine's parents were Fletcher, a sawmill superintendent, and Clara Bell, who followed the sawmill relocations throughout Alabama and Florida. Just one month after Parkhill's father, Dannitte, passed away, Katherine and Parkhill were married on June 20th, 1930 at the home of Parkhill's sister, Mamie, in Madison.[23] Parkhill was quite active prior to that time dating girls all over the state, particularly in Tampa, but also in Madison. He would speak early on about the times Monticello boys were literally chased out of Madison when they tried to date girls over there.

Throughout the 1930s, Parkhill owned Tuscawilla, passed down to him from his father, Dannitte, his maternal grandfather, G.W. Parkhill, and his maternal great grandfather, John M. Parkhill, who I will discuss later. Dannitte came to own Tuscawilla after paying off the mortgage encumbering the lands his wife, Emmala, had inherited from her parents. G.W. and his wife, Lizzie, had mortgaged Tuscawilla so that they could afford to establish and outfit a company of men in the Confederate army, which is also explained in greater detail in the Parkhill family chapter. A New Deal program called the Works Progress Administration provided the opportunity for many of the sharecroppers to leave the farms for jobs in the New Deal programs. It also led Parkhill to sell Tuscawilla in 1939 because many of the sharecroppers chose to leave the farm for the WPA.[24] My grandfather recalls that most people in the plantation areas came to know the WPA as 'We Piddle Around' instead of its intended name, the Works Progress Administration. Parkhill was able to buy four hundred acres of land in Miccosukee, a crossroads in Leon County, Florida, along with a large house included on the property.

Charles Parkhill Mays (left) and Claudia Katherine Bell (right).

Parkhill's wife, Katherine, as I mentioned, was almost 17 years old when the two were married. Despite being married so young, Katherine still managed to graduate from high school and attain her bachelor's degree at Florida State College for Women before having children. My grandfather remembers his mother completing her Master's Degree in English and starting to teach at Monticello High School, where she was the school's girls basketball coach in 1943.[25] On May 2, 1934, Charles Parkhill Mays and Katherine Bell Mays had Elizabeth Parkhill Mays, and just 20 months later on January 10, 1936, had my grandfather, Charles Parkhill Mays Jr.

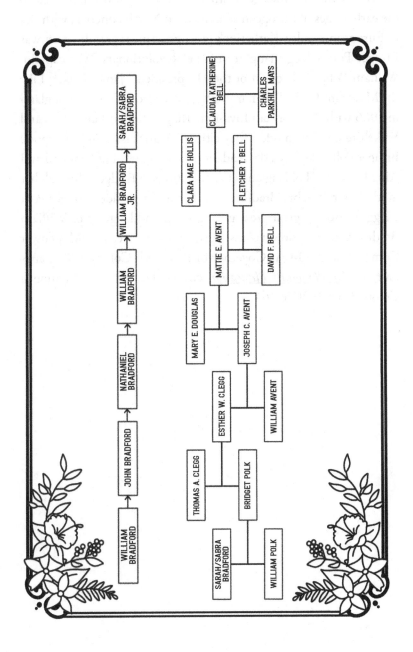

WILLIAM BRADFORD → JOHN BRADFORD → NATHANIEL BRADFORD → WILLIAM BRADFORD → WILLIAM BRADFORD JR. → SARAH/SABRA BRADFORD

CLARA MAE HOLLIS

CLAUDIA KATHERINE BELL

CHARLES PARKHILL MAYS

FLETCHER T. BELL

MATTIE E. AVENT

DAVID F. BELL

MARY E. DOUGLAS

JOSEPH C. AVENT

ESTHER W. CLEGG

WILLIAM AVENT

THOMAS A. CLEGG

BRIDGET POLK

SARAH/SABRA BRADFORD

WILLIAM POLK

27

Like Parkhill's lineage, Katherine's lineage also traces back to the early stages of European settlement in North America, with ties to European royalty. Katherine's great great great grandmother was Bridget Polk Clegg, daughter of the Revolutionary War captain, William Polk, and cousin of the 11th president, James Polk.[26] Like the Mays family, the Polk family also moved from France to England in 1066 with the Norman Invasion. They settled in Lancashire and Yorkshire near the modern-day cities of Manchester and Liverpool. Bridget Polk Clegg is a descendant of King James I of Scotland and King Edward III of England (15 generations to Bridget) through her mother, Sarah/Sabra Bradford. On her mother's side, Bridget Polk Clegg is also the great great great great granddaughter of William Bradford, a Mayflower passenger, signatory to the Mayflower Compact, and 30-year Governor of Plymouth Colony.[27] William's journal, *Of Plymouth Plantation* covers the affairs of Plymouth Colony from 1620 to 1646.

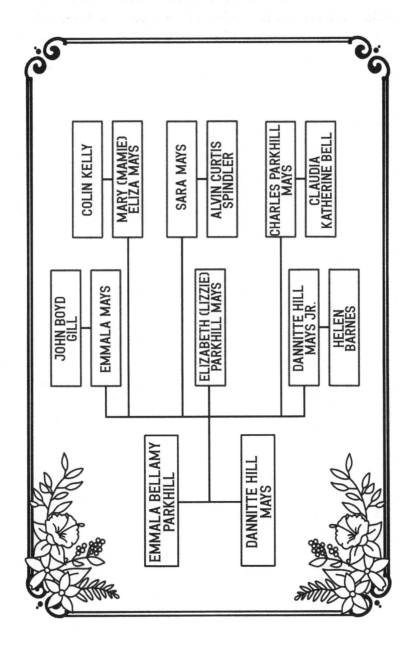

Of Dannitte Hill Mays and Emmala Bellamy Parkhill's six children, five were married and four have descendants living today.

(1) The eldest daughter, Elizabeth Parkhill (Lizzie), was never married.

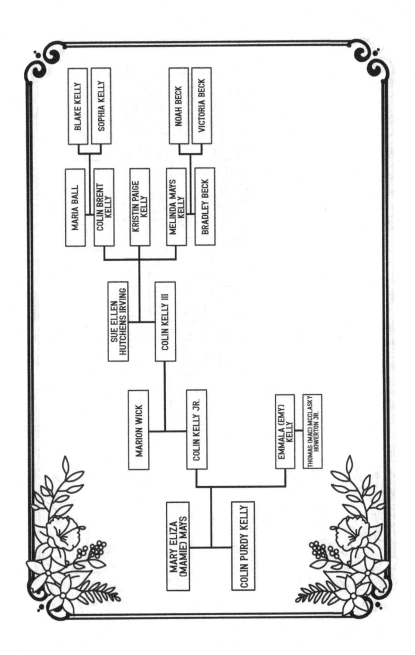

BLAKE KELLY
SOPHIA KELLY

NOAH BECK
VICTORIA BECK

MARIA BALL
COLIN BRENT KELLY

KRISTIN PAIGE KELLY

MELINDA MAYS KELLY

BRADLEY BECK

SUE ELLEN HUTCHENS IRVING

COLIN KELLY III

MARION WICK

COLIN KELLY JR.

EMMALA (EMY) KELLY

THOMAS (MAC) MCCLASKY HOWERTON JR.

MARY ELIZA (MAMIE) MAYS

COLIN PURDY KELLY

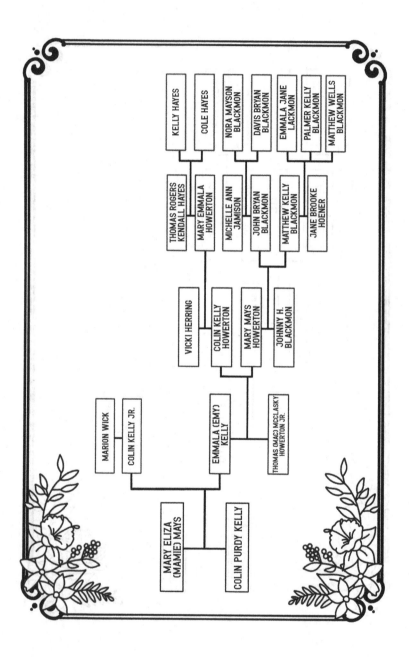

(2) Mary Eliza (Mamie) married Colin Purdy Kelly. They lived in Madison, Florida and had two children: Colin Kelly Jr. and Emmala (Emy) Kelly. Colin Jr. was a captain in the Army Air Corps and served in the Philippines in World War II. He was killed on December 10, 1941, just three days after Pearl Harbor, flying his B-17 on a patrol mission. The B-17 had just sunk a Japanese heavy cruiser with bombs, a feat not then accomplished by any air command, and was attacked by Japanese Zeros just 2 miles northeast of Clark Field. There is a marble statue in Four Freedoms Park in Madison, Florida honoring Colin Jr. as the first U.S. hero of World War II. He left behind a widow, Marion Wick, and a son, Colin III, who was offered entry to West Point at then president, Franklin D. Roosevelt's request after his father's noble service. Colin rejected this offer and elected to pursue the regular admissions process. Colin III was first married to Mary (Sue) Margaret Cooper, but after their divorce, married Sue Ellen Hutchens Irving. Colin and Sue have three children: Colin Brent Kelly, who married Maria Ball and had Blake and Sophia; Melinda Mays Kelly, who married Bradley Beck and had Noah and Victoria; and Kristin Paige Kelly.

This newspaper clipping from the August 21, 2020 issue of the *Jefferson Journal* features a writing piece by Colin Kelly Jr. from when he was in high school. It was originally in the Madison Enterprise-Recorder of January 22, 1932 as a winning entry spotlight. The piece, titled "The Citizen I Most Admire," highlights four essential characteristics that Colin Jr. said every good citizen must have.[28] It is a very interesting read—telling of his character and the man he went on to become. Note, particularly, the statement of the West Point Howitzer describing Colin's character and the follow up in the "profound words" section.

PASSING PARADE

Nelson A. Pryor
Guest Columnist

The Student

Can you imagine a time of student excellence? A time of student recognition? The *Madison* (Fla.) *Enterprise-Recorder*, of January 22, 1932, records such a time. Colin Kelly, Jr., posted his winning entry, "The Citizen I Most Admire" sponsored by the Madison P.T.A.. Spotlighted as follows:

"The Citizen I Most Admire"

"The Citizen I most admire has four salient characteristics, which if allowed to come to the front in everybody would make us all ideal citizens. I say allowed to come to the front because I personally think that everyone of us possesses them but because some other quality or qualities overshadows them they are not given an opportunity for full development.

"The first quality of the four is kindheartedness. This includes pleasantness, sociability and obligingness. Unless this person is pleasant, sociable and obliging he is not a good citizen. For to be a good citizen one must mix with his or her fellow citizens and they not only won't be inclined to do this but their fellow citizens won't want them to be around unless they are pleasant, sociable and obliging.

"The second of these qualities is good character. Let us consider the important characteristics of good character. Good character not only means honesty, truthfulness and the like, but it also embodies the golden rule, which is but honesty from a different angle. One may be honest in money matters and also with his time, but may be destroying his neighbor's property in an unintentional manner. The good citizen is careful not to do this.

"Next along the line of major characteristics comes that of good business judgment. Without this a citizen has no way of making money to put in his community enterprises. Don't misunderstand me. I don't mean that to be a good citizen one must have money or a big business. But with no business sense he would be a failure and failures are setbacks rather than aids to any community.

"Now last but not least by any means is that essential and lacking characteristic in so many citizens today. That of courage. Courage in business, courage in social affairs, (and needed of course,) courage in religious affairs. The courage to say yes or no, whichever your better judgment and conscience dictates at no matter what cost to your own interests. The citizen I most admire has

Photo Courtesy of Evelyn Lamb and Elmer C. Spear.
Colin Kelly

the backbone and courage to face a hostile crowd or even public sentiment and do what he thinks is right. How many men or women or boys or girls have we in this land of ours who would do this? How many real honest-to-goodness good citizens have we? While courage is not the only essential quality of a good citizen it is by far one of the most important. Without it no citizen can do the most for his community.

"In closing let me say that while many of us have seen many people who at a glance seem to be good citizens would they stand close inspection? The citizen I most admire will stand the closest inspection."

Howitzer

This bit of prophecy for Madison's Cadet Colin Kelly, Jr., was in West Point's 1937 Howitzer: "A combination of Irish blood and Southern sunshine has given Kelly the best qualities of both. Equally famous for his drawl and friendly smile. A temper, perhaps, but one that rises to defend the principles that he cherishes. He's positive in his opinions; vigorous in his actions. All-around ability and a knack of making friends bespeak a bright future for him, and those of us who really know him will be glad to say: 'I knew him when.'"

Profound Words

Writing of the death of Captain Colin P. Kelly, Jr., Curry "Tom" Merchant, *Enterprise-Recorder*, editor, penned: "The War (W.W.II) has come very close to home to us here, with one of our finest young men gone to a heroes death.

Colin's sister, Emy, married Thomas (Mac) McClasky Howerton Jr. Together, Emy and Mac have two children, Colin Kelly Howerton and Mary Mays Howerton. Mac also had three sons from a previous marriage, Tommy (deceased), Sandy, and Gaines. The greater family is extremely close. Colin Kelly Howerton married Vicki Herring and they have a daughter, Mary Emmala Howerton. She married Thomas Hayes and they have two children, Kelly and Cole Hayes. Mary Mays Howerton married Johnny H. Blackmon and they have two sons, John Bryan and Matthew Kelly Blackmon. John married Michelle Ann Jamison and they have Nora Mayson and Davis Bryan. Matthew married Jane Brooke Hoener and they have Emmala Jane, Palmer Kelly, and Matthew Wells. Through that lineage, specifically John Flood, Emy Kelly was admitted into the Colonial Dames (a prestigious organization of women who are descended from an ancestor who resided in the American Colonies before 1776) in 1960.[29]

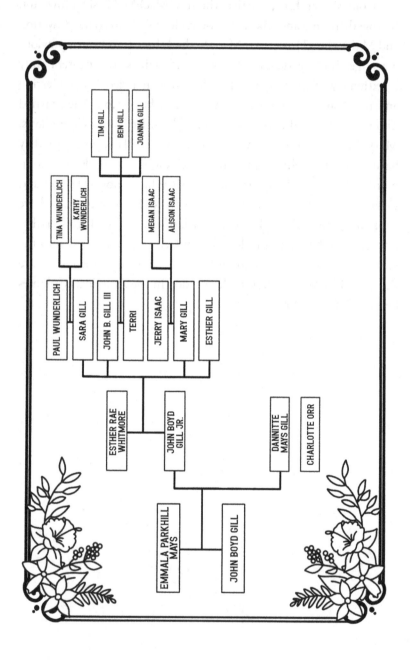

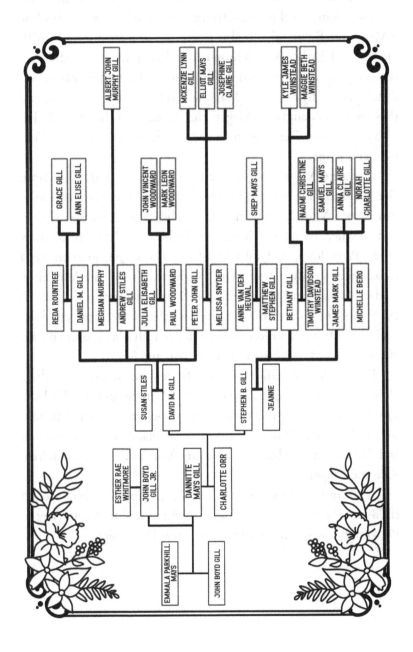

(3) Emmala Parkhill married John Boyd Gill and they have two sons, John Boyd Jr. and Dannitte Mays. John Boyd Jr. became a Methodist Reverend and also served in the navy during WWII. He married Esther Rae Whitmore, and they have four children: Esther; Sara, who is married to Paul Wunderlich and they have two daughters, Kathy and Tina; Mary, who is married to Jerry Isaac and they have two daughters, Megan and Alison; and Rev. John B. III, who is married to Terri Bergman and they have three children, Tim, Ben, and Joanna.

Dannitte Mays was an electrical engineer graduating from Georgia Tech. He married Charlotte Orr and they have two sons, Rev. David Murrah Gill. and Dr. Stephen Boyd Gill. Rev. David and his wife, Susan Stiles, have four children, Daniel Mark, Andrew Stiles, Peter John, and Julia Elisabeth. Daniel M. married Reda Roundtree and they have twin daughters, Grace and Ann Elise; Andrew Stiles married Meghan Murphy and they have a son, Albert; Peter John married Melissa Syder and they have three children, McKenzie, Elliot, and Josephine; and Julia Elisabeth married Paul Woodward and they have two sons, John and Mark.

Dr. Stephen B. Gill and his wife, Jeanne Brauer, have three children, Matthew, James, and Bethany. Matthew and his wife Anne van den Heuval have one child, Shep; James and his wife Michelle Bero have five children, Naomi, Samuel, Anna, Norah, and Thomas; and Bethany and her husband Timothy Winstead have two children, Kyle and Maggie.

(4) Sara Croom married Alvin Curtis Spindler, but had no children. The marriage was brief as Alvin, a well to do attorney in Pittsburgh, died early on during the Great Depression.

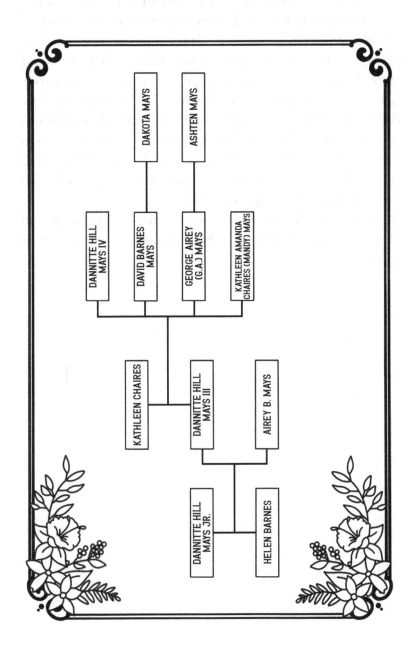

DAKOTA MAYS

ASHTEN MAYS

DANNITTE HILL MAYS IV

DAVID BARNES MAYS

GEORGE AIREY (G.A.) MAYS

KATHLEEN AMANDA CHAIRES (MANDY) MAYS

KATHLEEN CHAIRES

DANNITTE HILL MAYS III

AIREY B. MAYS

DANNITTE HILL MAYS JR.

HELEN BARNES

(5) Dannitte Hill Jr. married Helen Barnes and they had two sons: Dannitte Hill III and Airey B., who was never married. Dannitte Hill III, nicknamed Danny Boy, married Kathleen (Kitty) Chaires of the Benjamin Chaires' family, who is mentioned in the Bellamy family chapter as one of the men who helped survey Jacksonville. Danny Boy and Kitty have four children: Dannitte Hill IV, David Barnes, George Airey (G.A.), and Kathleen Amanda Chaires (Mandy). David has one son, Dakotah, who is a senior at Florida State University, and G.A. has one daughter, Ashten, who graduated from FSU and lives in Gainesville. Dakotah, G.A., and Ashten are the only living descendants.

(6) Charles Parkhill was the youngest child of Dannitte Hill Mays and Emmala Bellamy Parkhill and as mentioned, is my great grandfather.

CHAPTER THREE

The Parkhill Family

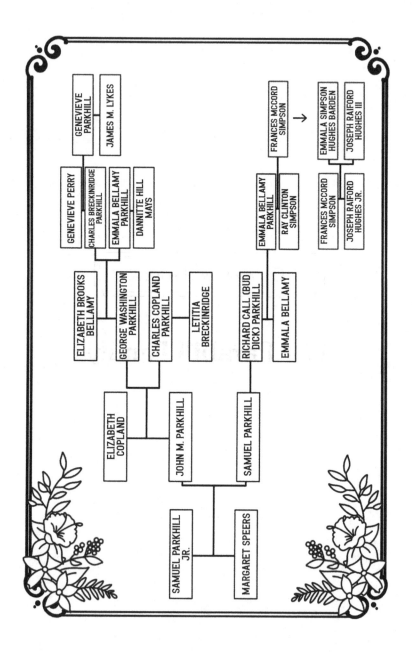

42

Another prominent lineage in my ancestral history is that of the first John Parkhill from Ireland and England. There is an old family story about the first John Parkhill and how he received his name. The story goes that in 1640, a French ship was wrecked in the English Channel and the only survivor was a child, who was afterwards adopted by an English family. The family decided to name the child "Parkhill" after the father's favorite place: "Park on the Hill."

As an adult, John Parkhill lived in Faversham, Kent, England and married an English woman. They had two sons who married Scottish wives forming the Parkhill lines of Glasgow and Paisley, Scotland. Both sons served as officers under William II, Prince of Orange, and one stayed in Scotland while the other settled in Londonderry. One of the great grandsons of John Parkhill from the Londonderry (Ireland) line of Parkhills was named John M. Parkhill Jr. after his great grandfather.[30] John M. Parkhill Jr. did not want to become a Presbyterian minister as was the tradition in his family, prompting him to run away to America.

After immigrating to New York in 1800, John became the owner of a hardware store in Richmond, Virginia and lived in one of the rooms above his shop. He would often rent the extra rooms to tenants as another source of income. John Holt Rice, a Presbyterian pastor at the First Presbyterian Church in Richmond, lived with his family as guests in John Parkhill's rooms for one summer. By the end of the summer months, John Parkhill had been converted by John Rice back to Presbyterianism. On January 31st, 1815, John Parkhill married Elizabeth Copland and converted her from an Episcopalian to a Presbyterian as well. In February of 1822, John and Elizabeth had a son: George Washington Parkhill (G.W.).

In 1827, John left for Florida with his brother-in-law, William Copland, and a group of Virginia migrants in search of land suitable for their families to live and farm on. In his diary John wrote, "I left Richmond in Virginia the evening of 15 April 1827 in company with William Copland with the view of visiting in Florida, examining the land & purchase if found of superior quality & the situation healthy."[31] It was comforting for John to see so many southerners from Virginia, North and South Carolina, and Georgia all in the same social class as he, and also making their way to that region of Florida. This familiarity helped John brave the increasing fear of migrating south to uncharted lands and he looked forward to the possibilities of fertile land and profits to be made.

After officially moving his family to Leon County, Florida, John began to establish Tuscawilla plantation and became very involved in banking and the community, serving as one of the founding members of Tallahassee's First Presbyterian Church.[32] John's brother Samuel purchased land on "Black Creek" just ten miles east of Tallahassee and William Copland settled nearby as well.

The charter for the Union Bank of Florida was proposed in February of 1833 and John Parkhill became its cashier. Interestingly, one of the only representatives on the Legislative Council who opposed the proposal was Abram Bellamy Jr., son of John (Jack) Bellamy. Abram Jr. was the uncle of John Parkhill's future daughter in law, Elizabeth Brooks Bellamy, who is discussed in greater detail later on.

After working at the bank for some years, John moved from Tuscawilla plantation to "Bel Air," a resort community he established south of Tallahassee, leaving his son, G.W., as owner of Tuscawilla.[33] When Yellow Fever hit middle Florida in 1841 even killing John's brother, Samuel, Bel Air became an escape for planters fleeing Tallahassee.

In the early 1840s, the Union Bank collapsed due to a stock trading alleged scheme. Both Tuscawilla and Bel Air were forcibly mortgaged, and John went into deep debt trying to fight for his property. John's dwindling psychological state caused by his brother's death and his financial perils led G.W. to return home from New York, where he was studying medicine, to manage Tuscawilla.[34] It is unknown if some of the debt eventually paid by Dannitte Hill Mays, husband of John's granddaughter, Elizabeth, came from the Union Bank plight.

All the while in Richmond, the migration to Florida, and throughout his life, John Parkhill had his trusted bondservant, James Page, by his side, and by the side of his wife and family. Page was well known and loved by the family and relied upon by John during travels as well as to operate Tuscawilla and Bel Air. Unusual for enslaved people, Page was literate and highly knowledgeable, and given extreme latitude in educating the plantations' slaves as well as others in the nearby countryside. Page also became an ordained minister, well respected by both the enslaved and free population, and was possibly one of the most well-traveled enslaved preachers in the antebellum south, preaching throughout Georgia, Alabama, Mississippi, North Carolina, and South Carolina, with connections all the way to West Africa. He even founded the Bethel Missionary Baptist Church just after the Civil War ended.[35]

In his recent book, *Father James Page: Enslaved Preacher's Climb to Freedom*, Florida A&M University Professor Larry Eugene Rivers "demonstrates the complexity of human relationships even in an institution as immoral as chattel slavery."[36] The book is well documented in finding letters and other writings by James Page focused on his life as an enslaved preacher and, later, as a free man. The writings allude to somewhat of a love-hate relationship between Page and the Parkhill family, blinded in some part by Page's devotion to John Parkhill, Parkhill's devotion to Page, and Page's sense of duty and allegiance. In short, Page was not one to publicly spout inflammatory ideas, but he did accomplish radical ends through his belief in black self-determination and independence.[37] He was revered throughout Florida for all he achieved and I recommend Professor Rivers' book for deeper insight into the life of this fascinating man.

Although the Parkhill family history alone is quite fascinating, it is the women who married into the Parkhill family that often bear the most significant historical lineage. Elizabeth Copland was born in September 1788 at Charles City, Virginia to Charles Copland and Rebecca Nicholson. At 12 years old, she was a student at the Bethlehem Moravian Seminary for Young Ladies in Pennsylvania.[38] A greater in-depth account of the Copland and Nicholson families is featured at the end of this chapter.

John and Elizabeth's son, G.W., attended medical school at the College of Physicians and Surgeons in New York City, known today as Columbia University School of Medicine, and began his practice in Tallahassee. Alongside his medical endeavors, G.W. also ran Tuscawilla Plantation and was highly active in public affairs before heading off to war. He was a member of the Florida House of Representatives from Leon County and Speaker of the House serving on several committees.[39]

As tensions were rising in the 1850s and the southern states discussed succession, there were conventions in each state to determine a plan of action. The Florida General Assembly voted to hold elections on December 22, 1860, to choose delegates for a state convention in Tallahassee on January 3rd, 1861.[40] G.W. Parkhill was elected to represent Leon County. The delegates were divided between immediatists—those who wanted to secede immediately— and cooperationists—those who wanted to wait and follow the lead of other states. G.W. was a staunch immediatist, believing that Florida needed to pave the way for the rest of the South, and by January 10th a majority came to agree with him. The next day the convention adopted the ordinance declaring Florida an independent state following South Carolina and Mississippi.[41]

On July 28th, 1858, G.W. married the exceedingly wealthy Elizabeth Brooks Bellamy (Lizzie), who brought a hundred slaves to Tuscawilla as her dowry. Lizzie's lineage was of multiple prominent families throughout Florida and South Carolina. Both the Brooks (Lizzie's maternal grandmother's family) and the Bellamy families will be discussed in chapters to come.

Interestingly, one of John M. Parkhill and Elizabeth Copland's other sons (G.W.'s brother), Charles Parkhill, was married to Letitia

Breckinridge, who was the sister of John C. Breckinridge, the candidate opposing Abraham Lincoln in the election of 1860.[42]

Lizzie and G.W. had their first child, Charles Breckinridge in 1859, just before the beginning of the Civil War, or the 'War Between the States' as Southerners called it. Their daughter and my great great grandmother, Emmala Bellamy Parkhill, was born on March 22, 1861 amidst the chaos of war. G.W. and Lizzie raised and funded an independent company named the "Howell Guards" after Maggie Howell, Confederate President Jefferson Davis' sister. They financially were able to support the company by mortgaging Tuscawilla and Lizzie worked with neighbors to personally sew the uniforms and outfit the entire company. G.W. became the Captain of Howell Guards serving alongside his cousin, Lt. Richard Call "Bud Dick" Parkhill. The company consisted of the officers and 98 enlisted men and was formally named the Second Florida Infantry upon reaching Richmond.[43] Bud Dick was G.W.'s cousin and the son of John Parkhill's brother, Samuel, who died of yellow fever in 1841. There is a strange old saying in the Parkhill and Mays families about Bud Dick that I have heard from my grandfather a number of times. It goes, "he's my uncle and my cousin so I call him Bud Dick." Although a comical remark, Bud Dick was actually Emmala Bellamy and Charles Breckinridge's uncle and cousin. I am still not sure about how the nickname Bud Dick came about.

Portrait of G.W. Parkhill.

G.W. was shot and killed when he was 40 years old at the Battle of Gaines' Mill, the largest of the Seven Days Battles defending Richmond that lasted from June 25 to July 1, 1862. Gaines' Mill was the first major victory of the war for both the Confederate army and the newly appointed commander, Robert E. Lee. As of June of 1862 Gaines' Mill was the second bloodiest battle in American history with 15,500 casualties, just behind the Battle of Shiloh.[44] Only a year later, the death rates at Gaines' Mill and Shiloh were overtaken by the approximate 50,000 deaths in the Battle of Gettysburg on July 1-3, 1863.[45] Appendix I to my grandfather's book, *Proud Heritage*, is, "The Life and Times of George Washington Parkhill (A.D. 1822-1862)," by Donald J. Ivey. This biography features pieces of the letters that G.W. wrote home to Lizzie while he was away fighting the war, describing many of the realities that the soldiers faced.

Prior to the battle, Bud Dick had lost a grey blanket, which a woman nearby replaced with a white one. Just before the fighting began, G.W. said to his cousin, "My soul, Dick, don't wear that white blanket; it will prove a target for the enemy. Exchange with me." G.W. took the blanket and wrapped it around himself as the cold persisted, and within minutes of the bugle call for battle, G.W. was one of the first shot down.[46] In an attempt to avenge his cousin, Bud Dick was also badly wounded, although not fatally. My grandfather recalls stories that his father told him about putting his fingers into Bud Dick's bullet hole as a child. The story passed down through the family, on to my grandfather, and then to me, said that Bud Dick was shot right after G.W. at Gaines' Mill as he marched up and down the breastwork cursing the Yankees for killing his cousin. Other sources say that he was shot days later at the Battle of Frazier's Farm. In Edward E. Baptist's book, *Creating an Old South: Middle Florida's Plantation Frontier before the Civil War,* he writes about G.W. 's death and the reaction of Bud Dick and the rest of the men in the regiment.

> Captain George Washington Parkhill lay face up in the growing daylight on the battlefield at Gaines' Mill. As the Confederate soldiers moved past his body, forward in Robert E. Lee's furious hammer blows against the Union flank, only the flies remained with him, settling on his gaping mouth and the wetness of his eyes. His cousin, Lieutenant Richard Parkhill, soon came rushing back. He had seen the fatal bullet's impact: 'When he fell it almost killed me. I was so much excited I scarcely knew what I was doing. The men over all wanted to lay down and they did so, when I walked down the line and told them to avenge their noble captain's death. Then the balls began to fall like rain, but they all gave a yell and started towards the enemy.'

After the battle ended, G.W.'s body servant, Lewis, apparently picked his body up and carried it into Richmond alongside Bud Dick and the other men in the regiment. While carrying the body, a man stopped the servant to ask whose body he was carrying, to which Lewis replied that it was Captain G.W. Parkhill of Florida and he was ordered to bring him into his house, the home where G.W. was born. The house was formerly owned by G.W.'s maternal grandfather, Charles Copland.[47] In the following days, Lizzie proceeded to bury G.W. at Shockoe Cemetery in Richmond before returning to Bel Air Plantation in Florida with her two young children.[48]

Genevieve Parkhill Lykes, daughter of Charles Breckinridge, further explains the lasting impact of G.W.'s death on her grandmother, Elizabeth Brooks Bellamy, in her book "Gift of Heritage," which I recommend reading as a primary source on the Parkhill and Lykes families. The Lykes family is best known for the Lykes Brothers Corporation, which was founded in the late 1800s by Howell T. Lykes in the Tampa Bay area. By 1910, Howell's seven sons joined the family operation and it was officially known as Lykes Brothers Inc.[49] Howell Lykes began the business with real estate, eventually expanding into other industries throughout Florida and Houston, Texas, such as shipping/steamship, cattle, banking, oil, and steel.[50] They became some of the largest landowners in America and one of the wealthiest families in the region. Genevieve Parkhill Lykes was married to James M. Lykes, one of the brothers who founded Lykes Steamship Lines out of Houston.[51]

After G.W.'s death, Emmala Bellamy Parkhill, known as Em, and her brother, Charles Breckinridge Parkhill, lived with their mother, Lizzie, at the home of her sister Emmala. Emmala was married to Bud Dick, and they all lived in a house that is still standing just east of the Jefferson County Courthouse on East Washington Street in Monticello, now referred to as the Turnbull house (pictured below). Interestingly, the courthouse is quite notable for being situated directly in the middle of the intersection of two major highways (U.S. 90 and U.S. 19) with a roundabout encircling it.

From the father she never knew, Emmala inherited the very temperament that may have been a contributing factor to G.W.'s death. Even when my grandfather knew her in her later years, he says she was a spitfire and a force to be reckoned with. She became a renowned leader in both her community in Leon and the surrounding Jefferson and Madison counties, and her home was the center of hospitality for people from all over the state.[52] Most people in Monticello came to know her as "Cousin Em" because, as my grandfather put it in his book, most of the older residents in Monticello were related one way or another, even if distantly, to which I will further explain later on.

In 1880, the Parkhill and Mays family lines converged through the marriage of Emmala and Dannitte Hill Mays. For the first five years of their marriage, Dannitte and Emmala lived in a white house on East Washington Street (pictured below), known as the Simkins house today. That house is right across the street from the house that Emmala and her brother grew up in, the previously mentioned Turnbull house. Both the Simkins house and the Turnbull house are listed on the national registry. In 1885, they would build their antebellum Victorian home on a one acre parcel a few blocks north and west of the Jefferson County Courthouse on North Olive Street. This would become the house that my grandfather would live in for the first seven years of his life and again during his high school years.

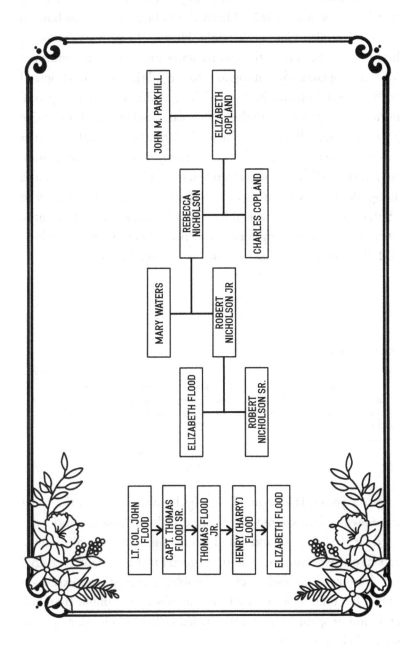

JOHN M. PARKHILL

ELIZABETH COPLAND

REBECCA NICHOLSON

CHARLES COPLAND

MARY WATERS

ROBERT NICHOLSON JR

ELIZABETH FLOOD

ROBERT NICHOLSON SR.

LT. COL. JOHN FLOOD

CAPT. THOMAS FLOOD SR.

THOMAS FLOOD JR.

HENRY (HARRY) FLOOD

ELIZABETH FLOOD

Returning to the Copland family, John M. Parkhill married Elizabeth Copland in 1815. Elizabeth's father, Charles was born in 1756 in Carolina County, Virginia. He was the fifth generation in his lineage to be born in the United States and a direct descendent of William Copland, who immigrated to Virginia in 1650 from England (father, Peter Copland Jr., born 1728; grandfather, Peter Copland, born 1700; great grandfather, Nicholas Copland Jr., born 1675; great great grandfather, Nicholas Copland, born 1638).[53] Charles was an eminent lawyer and doctor serving valiantly as a surgeon in the American Revolution. He studied law and medicine in Scotland alongside his brother-in-law, Dr. Robert Nicholson. From 1799 to 1801, Charles also represented Richmond in the House of Delegates. There are letters showing correspondence between Charles Copland and Thomas Jefferson one of which is featured below.[54]

From Thomas Jefferson to Charles Copland, 10 January 1801

To Charles Copland

SIR   Washington Jan. 10. 1801.

As I have occasion to write soon to mrs Randolph, I would ask the favor of you to take the trouble of informing me by a line what sum you have received from mr Grymes for her, what sum you have remitted, and whether she may expect soon any further & what remittance? which will oblige Sir

Your humble servt

TH: JEFFERSON

As a young lawyer in 1799, Charles also served as the court appointed defense counsel for the slave, Gabriel Prosser. Gabriel was tried for stealing a pig and found guilty of maiming a white man, a capital offense. However, Charles argued for the "benefit of clergy," which allowed Gabriel to choose public branding over execution only if he could recite a verse from the Bible.[55] The public branding and months spent in jail eventually led Gabriel to charge a massive slave rebellion in 1800.[56]

According to Meredith Henne Baker in *The Richmond Theater Fire: Early America's First Great Disaster*, the Copland family was deeply involved in the Richmond Theater Fire of 1811, which happened on the day after Christmas. It caused almost 100 deaths, including the Virginia governor. Charles was sound asleep in his home when he awoke to voices shouting "fire" and the sight of his home completely illuminated by the flames of the nearby theatre. As he jumped out of bed, his daughter, Elizabeth, ran home shrieking that the theater was on fire with her sister, Margaret, and brothers, Robert and William, inside. Charles ran into the front door of the burning theater to try and locate his children and wrote in his diary, "it was the most appalling sight I had ever witnessed." He ran through the building, screaming for Margaret and saving as many people as he could along the way.

> My daughter had worn to the theatre a cloth riding dress and...at the foot of the staircase, I passed my hand over the bodies of the females that lay prostrate before me, with a hope of discovering my daughter by the dress she had worn; for I had not time to examine faces, although there was a sufficient light... While I was passing my hand over their bodies looking for a cloth dress, I frequently with a loud voice called my daughter, hoping by loud speaking to rouse her or some one of them, but the power of speech was gone or impeded. None spoke, but other signs of life were not wanting.

Charles had to leave the building in the hopes that his children were waiting for him outside.[57]

Fortunately, both Robert and William were safe, however, 19-year-old Margaret perished among the flames. The tragic loss of his daughter sent Charles Copland into a depression so deep that people thought he had died. He spent five weeks at the family's second home in Muskingum County, Ohio, which was built on land that he was granted for serving as an army surgeon in the Revolutionary War. Charles's first wife, and Elizabeth's mother, was Rebecca Nicholson, of another prominent family in Virginia. Rebecca was born on August 3rd, 1766 in Williamsburg, Virginia and died in 1800 at only 34. Charles married a second time to Henigham Carrington Bernard, who was 25 years his junior.

The Nicholson House.

Rebecca Nicholson, lived with her family in Williamsburg, Virginia throughout the period before, during, and after the Revolutionary War. Rebecca (Becky) grew up in *The Nicholson House*, which was built between 1751 and 1753 and still welcomes visitors in Williamsburg today. Her mother was Mary Waters and her father was Robert Nicholson, a wealthy tailor. Robert's lineage traces back to the Colonial Burgesses through his mother, Elizabeth Flood. Elizabeth Flood's father was Henry (Harry) Flood, Henry's father was Thomas Flood II, Thomas' father was Capt. Thomas Flood I, and Capt. Thomas' father was Lt. Col. John Flood.[58] Lt. Col. John Flood came to America in 1610 on the ship "Swan" from Kent, England.[59] He served as a burgess for multiple Virginia counties, Speaker of the House of Burgesses in 1652, chairman of the Surrey County Commission, and was known as a Native American interpreter.[60]

Robert Nicholson and Mary Waters had seven children, some of whom became quite distinguished, including Robert Jr., who served as a surgeon in the Virginia Line of the Revolution alongside Charles Copland, and George, who became the two term mayor of Richmond, Virginia. For a brief time, Robert rented out rooms in the family home for additional income and in Williamsburg today, The Nicholson House is especially known for being haunted by a former tenant, Cuthbert Ogle. Ogle was a musician who emigrated from London in 1755 and stayed at the house for only two months before his death. Visitors claim that Ogle has touched them on the shoulder and that he is the source of scratching sounds throughout the house.[61]

By 1776, Robert sold his tailor shop to focus on civic responsibilities, however he and his family still resided in the rooms upstairs. Prior to the Revolutionary War, Robert served on the Committee for the City of Williamsburg, chosen December, 1774 with the prominent men, William Pasteur, John Minson Galt, George Wythe, and Peyton Randolph.[62] William Pasteur and John Minson Galt were doctors who opened up Pasteur & Galt Apothecary in Williamsburg in 1775. George Wythe is the nation's first law professor and was Thomas Jefferson's teacher. Peyton Randolph was the first president of the Continental Congress and a law professor at the College of William and Mary.[63]

CHAPTER FOUR

The Bellamy Family

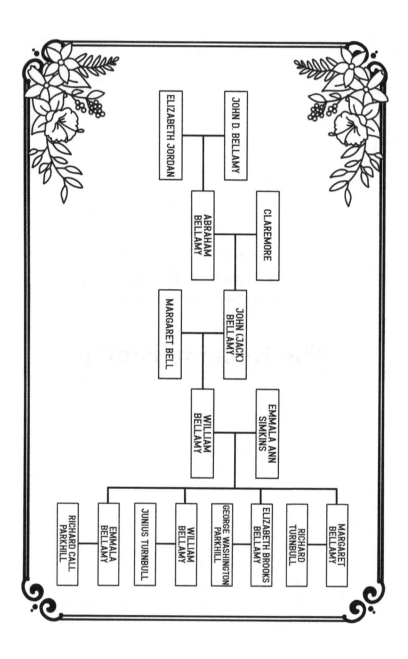

Both the Mays and the Parkhill family histories go hand in hand with the founding of many influential southern organizations throughout Virginia, South Carolina, and Florida. The Bellamy family, a direct line to the Mays and Parkhill families, is no exception to that feat. We must go back in time to begin tracing the Bellamys, although I have already mentioned the family multiple times. As stated at the end of the Parkhill family chapter, G.W. Parkhill married Elizabeth Brooks Bellamy, who was one of four daughters in the William Bellamy family line. I will discuss Elizabeth after exploring her ancestors both before and after immigrating to the United States.

The Bellamy family, originally spelled "Bell Ami" or "Bell Ame," traces back to 16th century France. After the Edict of Nantes was signed in 1598, Huguenots (French Calvinist Protestants) like the Bellamys were expelled from the country and forced to move to Holland, and other neighboring countries. John Bellamy, born in 1625, his wife, Martha Popham, and his son, John Bellamy Jr., moved to London, allowing both John and John Jr. to become a part of the gentry. John Jr., Sir John Yeamans, and many other English gentlemen were granted tracts of land around Charleston, South Carolina in 1665, directly by the Crown. Prior to becoming a very wealthy planter in South Carolina, John Jr. spent time at Plymouth Colony in Massachusetts and on the island of Barbados. John Jr. and his wife, Jane Horrell of Cornwall, England, had several sons as well.[64]

One of John Jr. and Jane's sons, John Bellamy III, settled on the Santee River in South Carolina. He too, like his father, became an extremely wealthy and extensive planter. In 1752, John III and his wife, Elizabeth Jordan, had a son, Abraham Bellamy, named for Elizabeth's father. Abraham, or Abram for short, served in the American Revolution as a Lieutenant in Marion's brigade from 1781 to 1782, and served under Andrew Jackson in the Spanish War.[65] Abram, his wife, Clara (or Claramond), and their children emigrated from South Carolina to Florida in 1819 when Andrew Jackson was governor of the new U.S. territory, and the family settled in an area called Cowford.

The Old St. Augustine Road, Tallahassee, FL.

In 1821, Abram, along with Benjamin Chaires and Francis Ross, surveyed a map of the area and decided to call the town Jacksonville after Governor Andrew Jackson. It is unclear if Abram's son Jack also participated in the survey. A few short years later in 1824, Jack was awarded the contract for what became known as the Bellamy Road, the first major U.S. federal highway in the Florida territory.[66] The road was called the Bellamy Road by those living in the Jacksonville area, and the St. Augustine Road by those living in the Tallahassee area. Part of it, known as the Old Bellamy Road, still exists and is in use today. There is a sign that reads:

> In 1824, the first session of the 18th United States Congress appropriated $20,000 to develop a public road in the Territory of Florida between Pensacola and St. Augustine. It was to follow as nearly as possible on the pre-existing old Mission Trail. The St. Augustine to Tallahassee segment was contracted to John [Jack] Bellamy. He completed this in 1826 using Native American guides and his own slaves. Remnants of the old sand road are used today and

part of the Bellamy Road forms the county lines between northwest Putnam and southwest Clay County.[67]

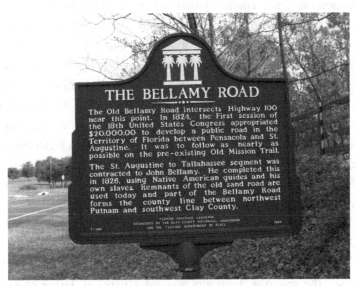

THE BELLAMY ROAD

The Old Bellamy Road intersects Highway 100 near this point. In 1824, the First session of the 18th United States Congress appropriated $20,000.00 to develop a public road in the Territory of Florida between Pensacola and St. Augustine. It was to follow as nearly as possible on the pre-existing Old Mission Trail.

The St. Augustine to Tallahassee segment was contracted to John Bellamy. He completed this in 1826, using Native American guides and his own slaves. Remnants of the old sand road are used today and part of the Bellamy Road forms the county line between northwest Putnam and southwest Clay County.

One of the signs at The Bellamy Road.

The road was quite expansive and continued to be a major highway until the Civil War when more modern roads were built around the area. Two miles of this road were very visible on land that was passed down to my grandfather's Aunt Lizzie and Aunt Sara, which was in turn eventually passed down to my great grandfather, Charles Parkhill Mays, and my grandfather, Charles Parkhill Mays Jr., and his sister, Elizabeth Mays Mills. The land was managed by Parkhill from the early 50s until he died in 1981, and Parkhill Jr. when Elizabeth's interest was sold in the mid-90s, and thereafter until 2006 when Parkhill Jr.'s interest was sold. The road served as a major landmark utilized for transportation along the family farms.

In 1798, Jack Bellamy married Margaret Bell, who had immigrated to Florida with him and his family. Together, they had five children: Abram Jr., Bethel, Elizabeth, Sarah, and William.

Abram Jr. became the first lawyer in Jacksonville, and later moved to St. Augustine. Abram Jr. and his wife, Elizabeth Ann Williams, had several children, two being Josephine and Theodosia Burr Bellamy. Theodosia married Thomas Jefferson Eppes, a Florida state senator, the great grandson of the third president, Thomas Jefferson, and a descendant of John Randolph of Roanoke. Josephine married Dr. John Wayles Eppes, the older brother of Thomas Jefferson Eppes'. John Wayles Eppes served as a lieutenant in the Howell Guards, the independent company raised by G.W. Parkhill and Elizabeth Bellamy.[68] Thomas Jefferson Eppes and Dr. John Wayles Eppes were sons of Francis Eppes, the grandson of Thomas Jefferson and the only surviving child of Thomas Jefferson's daughter, Maria Jefferson Eppes, and her husband, John Wayles Eppes. Growing up, Francis Eppes was quite close to his grandfather and many of his accomplishments were heavily influenced by the third president. After the death of his father and grandfather, Francis joined a group of Virginia migrants headed south to Florida in the late 1820s. Among the group of migrants was John Parkhill, father of G.W. Parkhill. In the same way that John Parkhill established Tuscawilla, Francis founded his family's plantation, L'Eau Noir (Black Water), and became a successful planter.[69]

The remainder of Jack Bellamy and Margaret Bell's family (excluding Abram) moved to Jefferson County. Jack and Margaret's first daughter, Sarah, married Colonel Burch, who initially surveyed the land where Bellamy Road would be built and awarded the contract to Jack to build the road.

For his work on the Bellamy Road, Jack was awarded land grants in addition to his previous acreage and became the owner of an 18,000-acre estate along the road just south of Monticello. He built a home for his family on the property and later established a private cemetery surrounded by a massive brick wall. The Bellamy Family Graveyard still exists today, although in a state of great disrepair as my grandfather recalls from his visit a number of years ago. The inscriptions on the tombstones, while somewhat recognizable, were badly faded with age. In the antebellum South, particularly Virginia, North Carolina, and South Carolina, family graveyards were often more commonplace than public cemeteries. Many of the settlers in Jefferson County, Florida, like the Bellamys, came from those states, bringing burial traditions and practices with them.

Photos of The Bellamy Plantation.

The Bellamy Plantation, which included the cemetery, the family home, and other plantation outbuildings, was passed down through the family, eventually to Margaret Bellamy Turnbull. The main home had two stories with great columns and was built on a high hill on the plantation with the cemetery south and west of it.[70] Only the graveyard remains on the site where the plantation home once stood and as of June, 1985, there are 57 marked graves still standing, 11 of which are missing tombstone inscriptions. Sharyn Thompson's report on the graveyard states:

> The graveyard is surrounded by a stucco-covered brick wall approximately 4'6" high..., with a simple, but beautiful hand wrought iron gate set in the center of the north wall. The wall measures approximately 121 feet on each of its four sides... In her book, The Bellamys of Territorial Florida, Eleanor Hortense Grenelle states that in searching through old documents she found a contract for the building of the brick wall that surrounds the Bellamy burying ground. 'This wall was to be built strong and durable and of the best brick, around a plot of two hundred feet square which had been set aside and signed by William Bailey, administer of the estate of John Bellamy, and Samuel L. Moore, the builder of the wall.'...All the graves within the walled yard are laid out in the east-west direction, with heads to the west, feet to the east. This follows the traditional belief that the dead will rise on Judgement Day facing the rising sun.[71]

Interestingly enough, it appears that some of the tombstones were actually placed at a much later date than the deaths occurred. Many of them include mistakes implying, as Sharyn Thompson says, "that whoever placed the stones and ordered the inscription cuts may not have been intimately involved with the deceased." An example of these presumed errors can be found on the grave of Abram Bellamy's wife, Clara. The name on her stone is marked as Claramond, while her name is actually Clara Mond (or Mund as written in Abram Bellamy's will). Additionally, both Abram and John Bellamy's stones are marked with the newer spelling of the name rather than the one they used on all legal documents: Bellame.[72]

Jack Bellamy became a successful planter and businessman, eventually becoming one of the wealthiest men in the whole State of Florida. By 1823, he served on the First Grand jury and issued the first marriage license in the county.[73] In addition to his business affairs, Jack wanted to provide an education for the children of the county and applied for a charter to form an Academy at Aucilla.[74] When he died in 1845, Jack left his home and much of his 18,000 acres of land to his youngest son, William, who was born on April 8, 1802 and who my lineage runs through.

In 1825, William Bellamy married Emmala Ann Simkins, who had connections to many prominent families from Edgefield: the Butlers, the Brooks, the Birds, and, obviously, the Simkins. William and Emmala had four daughters: Elizabeth (nicknamed "Lizzie" and "Daught"), Margaret, Emmala, and William, all of whom eventually became the most sought-after heiresses in all of Jefferson County and the adjoining counties. In 1846, shortly before his daughter William was born, William Bellamy died of "an inflammation of the lungs, induced by a violent cold," leaving all of his land and business affairs to his wife.[75] Emmala named her youngest daughter William to commemorate her husband since they bore no sons.[76] Heartbroken and worn out from running the plantation completely alone, Emmala died in 1851 at only 35 years old of "bilious pneumonia supervening upon a chronic pulmonary disease," leaving four young, very wealthy orphans behind.[77]

After William and Emmala's deaths, Emmala's sister, Elizabeth Simkins, took the two older daughters, Lizzie and Margaret, into her home.[78] Elizabeth Simkins was married to Monticello doctor, Waller

B. Taylor, and they lived in the house that would later become the old Dixie Hotel, a landmark in Monticello in the early 1900s. It burned when my grandfather was growing up. His sister, Elizabeth Mays Mills, and her husband, George, would build a home years later, on the site where the hotel once stood. This is where their children, York, Cornelia, and Scott, would grow up in their later years. Lizzie and Margaret stayed with their aunt and uncle until they left for college. The two younger daughters, Emmala and William, were cared for by their maternal grandmother, Behethland Brooks, who, in the next chapter, I will discuss in greater detail.

When it came time for marriage, the four daughters would marry into two families. Lizzie married G.W. Parkhill and Emmala married G.W.'s cousin, Richard Call Parkhill, better known as Bud Dick. Lizzie and G.W.'s children, Emmala and Charles, must have been the ones to come up with the saying, "he's my uncle and my cousin so I call him Bud Dick," because he was their uncle through marriage to their mother's sister, Emmala, and first cousin once removed through their father, G.W., who was Bud Dick's first cousin.

Emmala and Bud Dick had four daughters and a son whom they named after G.W. One of the daughters, Emmala Bellamy Parkhill (she had the exact same name as my great great grandmother who was her cousin), married Ray Clinton Simpson and had a daughter, Frances McCord Simpson. That daughter married Joseph Raiford Hughes Jr. and they had a son, Joseph Raiford Hughes III, and a daughter, Emmala Simpson Hughes Barden, who are very good friends of my grandparents' and also related, as one can see.

The other two daughters of William Bellamy and Emmala Ann Simkins, Margaret and William, married the Turnbull brothers. Margaret married Richard Turnbull, having eleven children and William married Junius Turnbull, having seven children. All four Bellamy daughters raised their families on plantations adjacent to each other left to them by their father, William.[79]

CHAPTER FIVE

The Butlers, The Brooks, The Birds, And Other Related Families

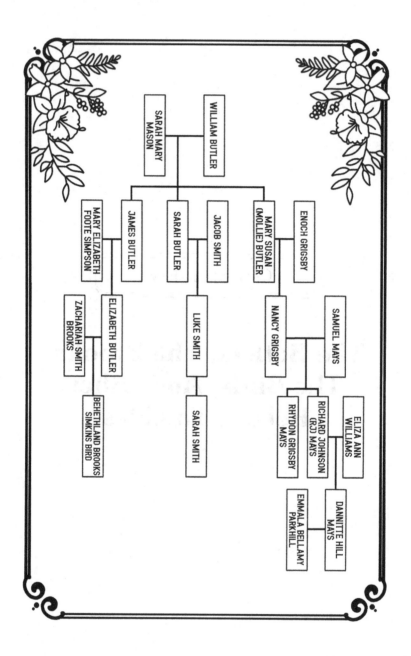

Even though the three families in my direct lineage are the Mays, Parkhills, and Bellamys, there are other notable families that are deeply intertwined in my ancestry. These families are also associated with the significant history of Edgefield and the development of both Jefferson and Leon Counties.

The Butler family was once one of the most ubiquitous names throughout Edgefield and the surrounding counties. The first evidence of the South Carolina Butlers in the United States was William Butler who supposedly immigrated to Virginia from Ireland in 1737.[80] According to Emma Plunkett Ivy's book, *As I Find it: A Partially Documented History of Some of the Butlers...*, the Butler family includes many significant figures throughout its history. She outlines the lineage from William Butler all the way back to Charlemagne, King of France from 768 to 816 and the first Holy Roman Emperor. Other esteemed ancestors include Arnald I, Duke of Flanders, who was grandson of Alfred the Great; Baldwin IV, Duke of Flanders and Artois, who was grandson of Berengarine II, King of Italy; Lady Matilda, who was wife to William the Conqueror; and Margaret, Princess of Scotland.[81]

Two of the most eminent American Butlers were William Butler's son, Captain James Butler, and Captain James' son, General William Butler Jr. Captain James Butler was born in 1738 in Virginia, moving to Edgefield as a child. He was one of three children of William Butler and Mary Mason, the other two being Sarah and Mary Susan (Mollie). Mollie Butler married Enoch Grigsby, as I previously stated in the Mays family chapter, and they were the parents of Nancy Grigsby. Nancy married Samuel Mays and two of their sons were Richard Johnson Mays (my great great great grandfather) and Dr. Rhyden Grigsby Mays, both previously mentioned. William Butler's other daughter, Sarah married Captain Jacob Smith and they had a son, Luke. Luke had a daughter, Sarah, who interestingly married Dr. Rhyden Grigsby Mays, making them distant cousins because they shared the same great grandparents.

My lineage runs through William Butler and Mary Mason

in a number of different ways. William and Mary Mason's son, Captain James Butler, married Mary Elizabeth Foote Simpson. According to the Brewster Family Pedigree, Mary Elizabeth Foote Simpson is supposedly a direct descendant of William Brewster, one of the passengers on the Mayflower, through the descendancy of his daughter Fear and her husband, Isaac Allerton. Though nothing is proven, in my research, I found the lineage to be through Fear and Isaac's daughter, Rose Allerton Tucker, through Rose's daughter, Jane Tucker Berryman, through Jane's son, Benjamin Berryman, and through Benjamin's daughter, Frances Berryman Foote, who was Mary Elizabeth Foote Simpson's mother.[82] The Foote family is also notable as they are known for being one of the oldest lines in Cornwall, England, where they held land prior to 1420.[83]

Capt. James Butler joined the "Snow Camp Expedition" in the American Revolution under Col. Richardson and led a company against the Cherokees under Col. Williamson. In 1779, he was arrested and imprisoned after refusing to swear allegiance to the British during the fall of Charles Town.[84] Just after his release, Capt. James and his son, James Jr., lost their lives in the Battle of Clouds Creek, also known as "The Bloody Scout," on November 17th, 1781. An account of the battle explains just how gruesome the encounter really was:

> After letting Colonel Williams and his Loyalists leave Edgefield County, Captain Stirling Turner camped at Clouds Creek. There had been a hard rain and all of the men were soaked. It was so wet that their guns were no longer able to fire. Turner had gone to the house of a Mr. Carter and had asked for food and a dry place to put their guns in order. Captain James Butler, Sr. advised Turner against stopping until they returned home. One of Butler's lieutenants suggested that they go to 'some secret place in the forest or swamp', but

Turner went against that advice. Major 'Bloody Bill' Cunningham's main force discovered where Turner's force was, and he struck Carter's house at daylight. The Patriots returned fire from the log cabin and sent out a messenger to ask for terms of surrender. Cunningham asked for the names of the men in the cabin...Captain James Butler, Sr. offered his own life for his son's, but James Butler, Jr. ended all discussion by firing his rifle out of the cabin and killing a Tory. A short fight ensued and James Butler, Jr. was killed. The Patriot militia saw that there was no hope of victory and surrendered, hoping for mercy. Cunningham did not show any, and he put the sword to Butler, Turner, and all but two men, Benjamin Hughes and Bartlett Bledsoe. Butler's body was cut up so badly that his wife was only able to identify him by the bible in his pocket. She put the parts of his body into a basket and then carried him off to be buried.[85]

Contrary to what the account above states, at the time of the battle, James' wife, Mary, and some of their children actually had smallpox. Nancy Butler, James and Mary's 16-year-old daughter who was not ill, went to the site of the massacre where her father, brother, and many friends had been killed to identify their bodies and assist in their burials.[86]

Capt. James's son, General William Butler Jr. served in the American Revolution as well and rose from Lieutenant to Major General. He avenged his father and brother's deaths through a surprise invasion on the very "band of Tories" under Major "Bloody Bill" Cunningham, so named for the bloody massacre of the Butlers and others at Clouds Creek.

In 1788, General William was chosen as a member of the South Carolina convention to vote on the adoption of the federal constitution, to which he voted against. That began his political career which included being a member of the Convention of 1790 that framed the state constitution, as well as being a 13-year member of Congress resigning only in favor of John C. Calhoun.[87] General William was married to Behethland Foote Moore, who was his first cousin and also a very important figure in South Carolina history. She was the daughter of Frances Foote and Captain Frank Moore. Frances Foote was the sister of Mary Elizabeth Foote Simpson, General William's mother, making the two first cousins.

Behethland Foote Moore was actively involved in the war, protecting her home and assisting soldiers passing through her town. At 15 years old, Behethland even volunteered to be a messenger in the middle of the night to warn a small force stationed on the other side of the Saluda River of danger.[88] The children of William and Behethland grew up to be prominent leaders as well. Pierce M. Butler was a governor of South Carolina, Emmala Butler married Waddy Thompson, a minister to Mexico, and Andrew Pickens Butler was a member of the US Senate.

My lineage runs through Elizabeth Butler, Capt. James' daughter and General William's younger sister, who was born in 1766 and married Zachariah Smith Brooks. My grandfather recalls that when my dad and my aunts and uncle were young, his aunt Lizzie would call my Uncle Brooks "Zachariah." At the time it was unclear why, but now he realizes that it was because Uncle Brooks shares a name with our ancestor, Zachariah Brooks.

Portrait of Zachariah Smith Brooks.

Zachariah was born in 1765 to Lieutenant James Brooks and Elizabeth Smith. He enlisted in the Revolutionary War as a teenager to fight alongside his brother and father. Interestingly, his brother, Elisha Brooks, was married to Elizabeth Butler's sister, Nancy Butler. Zachariah's war pension claim records state:

> Zachariah Smith Brooks enlisted in Newberry District, South Carolina 'shortly after the evacuation of Cambridge by General Greene' and served six months as a private in Captain John Wallace's company of South Carolina troops, and was in several skirmishes with the Tories. He served in 1781 and 1782 in Captain Joseph Towles' company. Colonel Samuel Hammond's South Carolina regiment was in a skirmish on the Edisto River, and was stationed about six weeks on the frontier guarding against the incursions of the Indians, also during this service he was detailed 'as one of the corps called the Life Guard of Pickens', length of service six months.[89]

Elizabeth and Zachariah had one son, Whitefield, and three daughters, Lucinda, Nancy, and Behethland.

Behethland Butler Brooks Simkins Bird, known by our family as "Old Aunt Het," was born on February 20th, 1793 in Edgefield, South Carolina. Her name in full is attributed to both of her parents, as well as both of her husbands. She was born Behethland Butler Brooks—Butler is her mother's maiden name and Brooks is her father's surname. The origin of the peculiar name "Behethland" is actually from Capt. Robert Behethland of Jamestown, Virginia.[90] Behethland's first marriage was to a Simkins and her second to a Bird. She connects many of my family's ancestral lines: her parents merged the Butler and Brooks families, she then connected to the Simkins and Bird families through marriage as I will explain further. Her daughter married into the Bellamy family, her granddaughter married into the Parkhill family, and her great-granddaughter married into the Mays family. Behethland is my five times great grandmother twice, directly related to both my grandfather through the Mays-Parkhill-Bellamy-Simkins lineage and my grandmother through the Carmichael-Bird lineage.

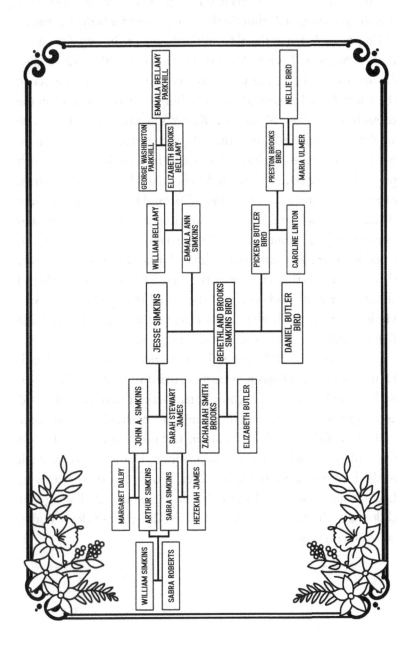

Behethland's first marriage was to Jesse Simkins in 1810. Jesse was the grandson of Arthur Simkins, renowned for being the Father of Edgefield. A sign at the old Simkins Cemetery in Edgefield states that Arthur was "Born in Virginia on December 10, 1742, he died September 29, 1826. He was a county court judge, a member of the South Carolina general assembly [for 20 years], and was on the commission to divide Ninety-Six District into counties."[91] He was also a delegate to the convention that adopted the federal Constitution, but originally voted against it because he believed it took too much power from the states.[92] Jesse and Behethland had several children, one being Emmala Ann Simkins, who would later marry William Bellamy. Emmala and William unfortunately died quite early, and as previously mentioned in the Bellamy family chapter, Behethland cared for their two youngest daughters, Emmala and William, upon their parents' deaths. Jesse Simkins died in 1821 leaving Behethland about 40 acres of land on which she would later build her home.[93] He is buried at the Butler family cemetery in Edgefield alongside Behethland's parents, Zachariah and Elizabeth.

On August 17, 1827, Behethland married her second husband, Daniel Bird. Daniel was previously married to Sarah Wells Oliver, with whom he had one daughter. After Sarah's death, Daniel served as a captain in the War of 1812 and was married a second time in 1814 to Behethland's older sister, Lucinda, with whom he had five children.[94] While married to Lucinda, Daniel served as clerk of the Edgefield County Court. After nearly 14 years of marriage, Lucinda died and Daniel and Behethland wed in 1827 having four children of their own: Daniel Butler, Sarah Oliver, Pickens Butler, and William Capers.

With the 40 acres of land left to her by Jesse Simkins, Behethland and Daniel built their home, Oakley Park, in Edgefield in 1835. This structure still exists today as the Oakley Park Museum (pictured above).[95] On October 30th, 1840, just a few years after the home's completion, Daniel's son, Thomas, (from his second marriage to Lucinda) was killed in a shooting incident at the Edgefield County Courthouse.[96] Thomas's first cousin was Preston Smith Brooks, a member of the US House of Representatives and known for being one of the most polarized figures in the decade before the Civil War. He was characterized for his undisciplined and often violent behavior, which contributed to the death of his cousin.[97] There was a disagreement between Preston Brooks and Col. Lewis T. Wigfall, based on a defaming comment that Wigfall made about Preston's father, Whitefield Brooks (brother to Behethland). It is unclear exactly how the event occurred, but somehow Thomas was shot by Wigfall at the Edgefield County Courthouse in place of Brooks.[98]

Immediately after the incident, Daniel sold Oakley Park and the family moved to Monticello. Daniel first bought Bunker Hill plantation from Needham Bryan, which was built on a high hill along the northern mail route from Thomasville, Georgia, to Monticello.[99] Daniel later also bought Nacoosa plantation (pictured below), two miles south of Monticello, from William Bellamy. In 1850, about 10 years after the death of their son, Thomas, a tragic accident happened at Nacoosa. Behethland and Daniel's daughter, Sarah Oliver, named for Daniel's first wife, was 19 years old and recently engaged. She fell asleep while reading by an open fire outside the house and was so badly burned that she died just a few days later.[100] Daniel and Behethland died within months of each other between late 1864 and early 1865.

CIRCA 1907, Four families: Bird family, Ball family, Brooks family, and Burroughs family gathered after the death of Pauline Bird Burroughs. Identified are from left, teenage boy: Oliver Burroughs, man on his right: Oliver Burroughs Sr., man in uniform: Preston Bird. Middle on stairs above: Caroline Brooks Bird, two teenage girls below: Emila Bird Burroughs & Pauline Bird Burroughs (later Blois), bottom step right, tiny boy: William Ball, middle of stairs: Archie Burroughs holding a dog. Right side: lady is Emila Bird Ball, right side John Ball.[101]

The two Bird plantations, Nacoosa and Bunker Hill, stayed within the family even after Daniel and Behethland's deaths. In 1857, William Capers married Caroline Brooks and they inherited and lived at Nacoosa. Daniel Jr. first married Virginia Butt, with whom he had two children, and then married Catherine Dilworth, with whom he had two more children. Daniel Jr. inherited Bunker Hill and the home remained in his family for years after. Pickens, who my lineage runs through, also bought a plantation from Needham Bryan in the town that is now known as Drifton naming it Treelawn after the large oak trees on the front lawn. He lived there with his wife, Caroline Linton. The house that currently stands where Treelawn once stood is pictured below. Pickens and Caroline's children were Preston Brooks, Sarah Behethland, Ella, Jane, and Daniel. In 1861, Pickens joined the Confederate army serving as a lieutenant and, later, captain in the third and tenth Florida regiments. He was wounded at Cold Harbor in 1864 and died a few days later leaving Caroline and oldest son, Preston Brooks, to care for Treelawn.[102]

Preston Brooks Bird built a home on the southern end of Treelawn and lived there with his wife, Maria Ulmer. Although Preston Brooks died in 1932, he was a legend long after and my grandfather remembers him as a notable character well-known around Monticello. One of Preston's brothers, Daniel B. Bird, was a two-term sheriff serving when the present Courthouse was built. Daniel married Elizabeth Ulmer, sister to Preston's wife, Maria, and their only son, Thomas Buckingham Bird, was a Jefferson county judge. Born in 1892, Thomas Buckingham Bird, went to the University of Florida for both his undergrad and law degree before volunteering for the army during World War I. He was commissioned as a second lieutenant and eventually promoted to captain serving in Europe and receiving honorable discharge on December 10, 1918. In 1919, Thomas Buckingham became a Monticello lawyer and in 1921, he became the Jefferson County Judge.[103] His son, Thomas Buckingham Jr., following in his father's footsteps was also the respected Jefferson County Judge. Thomas Buckingham Jr.'s son, Thomas Buckingham Bird III, was a high school classmate and friend of my grandfather and they remain close today. Although never a County Judge, Thomas Buckingham Bird III graduated from Florida Law School and is the County Attorney for Jefferson County in addition to his law practice. He served as School Board Attorney for many years as well as City Attorney. He married Beulah Brinson Bird, who is also a close friend today, and a longstanding member and president of the Jefferson County Historical Association. They are both contributors to this book.

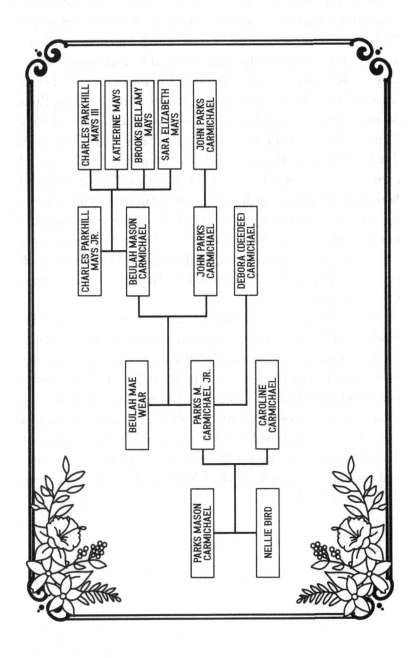

CHARLES PARKHILL MAYS III

KATHERINE MAYS

BROOKS BELLAMY MAYS

SARA ELIZABETH MAYS

JOHN PARKS CARMICHAEL

CHARLES PARKHILL MAYS JR.

BEULAH MASON CARMICHAEL

JOHN PARKS CARMICHAEL

DEBORA (DEEDEE) CARMICHAEL

BEULAH MAE WEAR

PARKS M. CARMICHAEL JR.

CAROLINE CARMICHAEL

PARKS MASON CARMICHAEL

NELLIE BIRD

Preston Brooks and Maria Ulmer had five daughters and three sons, all of whom were very close according to a 1984 interview of Parks M. Carmichael Jr. One of their sons, John (Johnny) Ulmer, was a Pinellas county judge who practiced in Clearwater, Florida and was well respected state-wide.[104] One of their daughters, Nellie, married Parks Mason Carmichael and they had two children, Parks Mason Jr. and Caroline (Aunt Caroline to my grandmother, Mason). Caroline lived in Washington DC with her husband, Lee Jackson. The family lived in Monticello before moving to St. Petersburg and eventually returning to Drifton. In the interview, Parks Jr. described how his father divorced Nellie and left their family when he was only six years old. Parks Sr. was originally from McDonough, Georgia, but moved to Mexico after their divorce and never had a relationship with or financially supported the family again.[105] With no official job training of her own, Nellie established "Milady's Shop" and operated it for many years.

As I briefly explained in the first chapter, Parks lived with his mother and sister in Drifton until eighth grade when he moved to his Aunt Lula and Uncle Sidney Robertson's home in Gainesville. He only studied for two years as an undergraduate and two years in law school at the University of Florida before being admitted to the Florida Bar his senior year. Nellie was able to support their family of three, but Parks explained that he was only able to afford college by working constantly since age 13 and with the help of his Bird aunts and uncles. Parks cites his uncle, Johnny, as one of his inspirations for pursuing law.[106]

Mason Carmichael as a child.

In 1929, Parks married and had a daughter, Debora (DeeDee). He was divorced in 1935 and then married Beulah Mae Wear in 1937. They had my grandmother, Beulah Mason Carmichael, now Mays, in 1939, and her brother, John Carmichael, in 1941. John has a son, John Jr., who currently lives in the Washington D.C. area.

CHAPTER SIX

Descendents

In officially beginning my research for this book some months ago, I quickly noticed the deep impact that the women in these families had on their kin and on their communities. Women like Rebecca Nicholson, Elizabeth Copland, Elizabeth Brooks Bellamy, and Emmala Bellamy Parkhill all came from more significant historical backgrounds than did their husbands. Despite the patriarchal structures they were born and raised into, they managed to make their names and their influence known throughout the State, as well as in family stories passed down through generations and in written stories that reach beyond the times in which they lived. Frankly, I find it amazing just how much they all accomplished in spite of the impediments of their times.

I also noticed that the tight knit communities of Edgefield and Monticello were deeply intertwined. Everyone seemed to be related in some way whether it be through marriage or through kinship. In the early 19th century in Edgefield, the Butler, Brooks, and Simkins families were prominent and many could trace roots back to one or all of the three. As time went on, people moved on to other small towns and cities throughout the still new and unsettled country. Those like R.J. Mays and Eliza Ann Williams, John Parkhill and Elizabeth Copland, Abram Bellamy and Claramond, and Daniel Bird and Behethland Brooks would pick up their families and build a new life for themselves in an uncharted region of the country. They would build Monticello and the surrounding Florida towns from the ground up and would settle the area with their own descendants. My grandparents came from those descendants and are actually fifth cousins, sharing Behethland Brooks (Simkins Bird) as a great great great grandmother.

Small towns like Monticello make up our nation just as big towns and cities do. It is truly fascinating to view the history of these places through the lens of individuals. Although personal knowledge becomes depleted after so many generations and one may never fully understand who their distant ancestors were beyond their written accomplishments, I can understand my grandparents and they can understand their grandparents. We can pass down stories and memories to each new generation. To trace these connections, not only between families, but between my ancestors and myself, is incredibly special. Ordinary people like those I have written about and others like them make up the foundation of this nation— and ordinary women like Rebecca Nicholson, Elizabeth Copland, Elizabeth Brooks Bellamy, and Emmala Bellamy Parkhill played a larger role in history than many may realize.

Epilogue

After writing about my family for quite some time now, I have come to understand three important things about the past. One: who we are is often determined by the actions and decisions of those who came before us. Two: social standards are created and normalized by individuals. Three: history is better understood when it is observed with a retrospective lens.

Learning about my family has helped me better understand my past, my family's past, and guidelines for my future. I hope this book has inspired its readers to look into their past, and find where and who they came from. It may, very well, alter the way they see the world.

I want to close this book with a card my mom recently found that was given to my dad and her by my great grandmother, Katherine Bell Mays. It is a note thanking my parents for travelling down to Tallahassee for her 80th birthday party in 1993. It reads:

Dear Lisa and Parkhill,

Thank you so much for the beautiful vase with lilies! You were sweet to pick out such a lovely present for me.

I want to thank you all for taking the trouble and expense to travel all the way to Tallahassee to be at my birthday party, I was duly impressed!

I also enjoyed being with you on the ancestor's grave hunt [Bellamy Graveyard], you should know who you come from!

I love you,
Grandmother Mays

If there is anything to take away from this book, it is my great-grandmother's words: *"you should know who you come from."*

Monticello, Florida 32344
July 13, 1993

Dear Lisa and Parkhill,

Thank you so much for the beautiful vase with lillies! You were sweet to pick out such a lovely present for me.

I want to thank you all for taking the trouble and expense to travel all the way to Tallahassee to be at my birthday party. I was duly impressed!

I also enjoyed being with with you on the ancestor's grave hunt, you should know who you come from!

I love you
Grandmother Mays

ENDNOTES

1   "Interview with Parks Carmichael, July 27, 1984" by Sid Johnston, *University of Florida College of Law Oral History Collection, Samuel Proctor Oral History Program (SPOHP)*. Transcript. https://ufdc.ufl.edu/ UF00006321/00001/1x (accessed May 1, 2020).

2   *South Carolina Magazine of Ancestral Research, Vol. VII, No. 4* (Fall 1979), 234.

3   Samuel E. Mays and Samuel E. Mays, *Genealogy of the Mays Family and Related Families to 1929 Inclusive* (Salem, MA: Higginson Book Company, 2006).

4   Phil Heard, *THERE CAME A MAN: The Life and Influence of Richard Johnson Mays On the Development of Baptist Work in Florida.* (Madison, FL: Florida Baptist Historical Society, 2004).

5   David Neff. *Sign Erected at Site of the Church of Rev. Mease.* Photograph. Hampton, VA: July 10, 2011. Ancestry. https://www. ancestry.com/mediaui-viewer/collection/1030/tree/16419899/ person/19275392224/media/9e4d7eeb-5572-455e-a7fe-f9be3ae648eb? phsrc=ALT17&usePUBJs=true (accessed April 15, 2020).

6   Louise Pledge Heath Foley, *Early Virginia Families Along the James River: Henrico County, Goochland County, Virginia* (United States: Genealogical Publishing Company, 1992).

7   Mary Denham Ackerly and Lula Eastman Jeter Parker, *"Our kin"; the genealogies of some of the early families who made history in the founding and development of Bedford County, Virginia.* (Lynchburg, VA: J.P. Bell Co., 1930).

8   Mattox Mays. "[Last will and testament of Mattox Mays.]" Recorded in Virginia Deed Book 1 1752-1759, p. 15. Halifax County, VA: August 16, 1772. (accessed May 2, 2020).

9   Dorcas Abney Mays Hill. "[Last will and testament of Dorcas Abney Mays Hill.]" Recorded in Will Book B, p. 194 & 195. Edgefield, SC: Office of W.J. Kincaid, Probate Judge, 1804. (accessed May 2, 2020).

10 John Bennett Boddie, *Virginia Historical Genealogies* (United States: Genealogical Publishing Company, 2009).

11 Phil Heard, *THERE CAME A MAN*.

12 A. L. McDuffee, Historian General, NSDAR, "Lineage Book, Vol. 097" (Washington, DC.: Press of Judd & Detweiler, 1927). Accessed September 21, 2020, https://www.ancestry.com/imageviewer/collections/61157/images/46155_b290237-00005?usePUB=true&phsrc=OBT1&usePUBJs=true&pId=2693283.

13 Phil Heard, *THERE CAME A MAN*.

14 "Richard J. Mays," accessed July 20, 2020, https://floridabaptisthistory.org/richard-j-mays/.

15 C. Parkhill Mays Jr., "letter to Mrs. Linda Gramling Demott," (Lakeland, FL: March 16, 2000).

16 H. G. Cutler, *History of Florida*.

17 Phil Heard, *THERE CAME A MAN*.

18 "MAYS, Dannite Hill (1852-1930)," Biographical Directory of the U.S. Congress - Retro Member details, United States Congress, accessed August 19, 2020 https://bioguideretro.congress.gov/Home/MemberDetails?memIndex=M000289.

19 Dannitte H. Mays. *The Pensacola Journal, Vol. XI - No. 23*, "Hon. D.H. Mays, of Monticello, a Candidate for Congress." January 26, 1908. From Library of Congress. https://chroniclingamerica.loc.gov/lccn/sn87062268/1908-01-26/ed-1/seq-1/#date1=1908&index=5&rows=20&words=Dannitte+Mays&searchType=basic&sequence=0&state=Florida&date2=1918&proxtext=dannitte+mays&y=0&x=0&dateFilterType=yearRange&page=1 (accessed August 19, 2020).

20 Dannitte H. Mays. *The Pensacola Journal, Vol. XI - No. 23*.

21 Dannitte H. Mays. *The New Enterprise (Madison, FL), Vol. VII - No. 33*, "The Mays' Platform." April 16, 1908. From Library of Congress. https://chroniclingamerica.loc.gov/lccn/sn95047178/1908-04-16/ed-1/seq-1/#date1=1908&sort=date&rows=20&words=D+H+MAYS&searchType=basic&sequence=0&index=0&state=Florida&date2=1918&proxtext=%2d.h.+mays%22&y=0&x=0&dateFilterType=yearRange&page=2 (accessed August 19, 2020).

22 Dannitte H. Mays. *The Pensacola Journal, Sunday Morning Edition*, "For Congress, D.H. Mays For Re-election." May 8, 1910. From Library of Congress. https://chroniclingamerica.loc.gov/data/batches/fu_emerson_ver01/data/sn87062268/00295865088/1910050801/0320.pdf (accessed August 19, 2020).

23 Mays, C. Parkhill Jr., *Proud Heritage: From the Early Settlers of Florida to the Present* (Lincoln, NE: iUniverse, 2007).

24 Mays, C. Parkhill Jr., *Proud Heritage.*

25 Mays, C. Parkhill Jr., *Proud Heritage.*

26 L. R. Spencer, Registrar General, NSDAR, "Lineage Book, Vol. 161" (Washington, DC.: Press of Judd & Detweiler, 1938). Accessed September 25, 2020, https://www.ancestry.com/imageviewer/collections/61157/images/46155_b290463-00188?pId=3741526.

27 W. Harold Broughton, *The Cleggs of Old Chatham: the Ancestry, Family, Descendants of Thomas A. Clegg & Bridget Polk: Their Kin & Events of Interest* (Charlotte, NC: The Association, 1977).

28 Nelson A. Pryor. *Jefferson Journal, Vol. 14 No. 4, sec. Viewpoints and Opinions,* "Passing Parade." August 21, 2020.

29 Emy Mays Kelly, *Application for Membership to the National Society of the Colonial Dames of the XVII Century, Dominie Everardus Bogardus.* (Tallahassee, FL: May 25, 1960).

30 Genevieve P. Lykes, *Gift of Heritage* (Self Published, 1969).

31 John Parkhill. *Parkhill Diary, Folder 11.* Diary. From The Southern Historical Collection at the Louis Round Wilson Special Collections Library, University of North Carolina, *The John Parkhill Papers, 1813-1891.* https://finding-aids.lib.unc.edu/01826/ (accessed April 15, 2020).

32 Genevieve P. Lykes, *Gift of Heritage.*

33 Edward E. Baptist, *Creating an Old South: Middle Floridas Plantation Frontier before the Civil War* (United States: The University of North Carolina Press, 2003).

34 Edward E. Baptist, *Creating an Old South.*

35 Larry Eugene Rivers, *Father James Page: An Enslaved Preacher's Climb to Freedom* (United States: Johns Hopkins University Press, 2021).

36 Bob Holladay. *Tallahassee Democrat,* "FAMU Professor Tells Complex Story of Enslaved Preacher in 'Father James Page' | Holladay." February 5, 2021. https://www.tallahassee.com/story/life/2021/02/05/famu-professor-book-tells-complex-story-enslaved-preacher-james-page-bethel-missionary-baptist/4396546001/ (accessed February 10, 2021).

37 Larry Eugene Rivers, *Father James Page.*

38 William Cornelius Reichel, *A History of the Rise, Progress, and Present Condition of the Bethlehem Female Seminary, with a Catalogue of Its Pupils, 1785-1858* (Philadelphia: Lippincott, 1858).

39 Mary Oakley McRory and Edith Clarke Barrows, *History of Jefferson County, Florida* (Monticello, FL: Pub. under the auspices of the Kiwanis Club, 1958).

40 Ralph A. Wooster. *The Florida Historical Quarterly 36, no. 4, 373-85*, "The Florida Secession Convention." 1958. www.jstor.org/stable/30139845 (accessed June 8, 2020).

41 Edward E. Baptist, *Creating an Old South.*

42 Morris, *The Florida Handbook*, p. 616; E.B. Long, *The Civil War Day by Day*, p. 1-2; and Rerick, *Memoirs of Florida*, 1:644 (New York: Da Capo Press, 1971).

43 *Tallahassee Democrat*, "Parkhill Led Tallahassee Regiment in War." March 28, 1974.

44 "Gaines' Mill," American Battlefield Trust, April 17, 2020. https://www. battlefields.org/learn/articles/gaines-mill.

45 Eric Milzarski, "Here Are 6 of the Deadliest Battles Ever Fought," Business Insider, February 25, 2019. https://www.businessinsider.com/ here-are-6-of-the-deadliest-battles-ever-fought-2018-2.

46 Genevieve P. Lykes, *Gift of Heritage.*

47 *Tallahassee Democrat*, "Parkhill Led Tallahassee Regiment in War."

48 Sharyn M. E. Thompson, *The Bellamy-Bailey Family Graveyard* (Tallahassee, FL: Jefferson County Historical Association, 1985).

49 Diana J. Kleiner, *Handbook of Texas Online*, "LYKES BROTHERS," accessed August 5, 2020, https://www.tshaonline.org/handbook/entries/ lykes-brothers.

50 Diana J. Kleiner, *Handbook of Texas Online.*

51 *Tampa Tribune*, "Widow Of James Lykes Dies In Texas At 85." January 6, 1971.

52 *Tallahassee Democrat*, "Mrs. D.H. Mays Taken By Death in Monticello." May 21, 1954.

53 Luginbuel Funeral Home, "Descendants of William Copeland," accessed August 5, 2020, http://assets.luginbuel.com/genealogy/documents/ Copeland,%20William%20Family.pdf.

54 *Thomas Jefferson to Charles Copland, 10 January 1801.* Letter. From National Archives, *Founders Online, Jefferson Papers*. https://founders. archives.gov/documents/Jefferson/01-32-02-0306 (accessed April 10, 2020). [Original source: Barbara B. Oberg. *The Papers of Thomas Jefferson, vol. 32, 1 June 1800–16 February 1801*. Princeton: Princeton University Press, 2005, p. 421.]

55 Bert M. Mutersbaugh, *The Journal of African American History, No. 2 ed., Vol. 68: The Background of Gabriel's Insurrection* (Washington, DC: Association for the Study of African American Life and History, 1983), doi:https://doi.org/10.2307/2717723.

56 "Africans in America/Part 3/Gabriel's Conspiracy" retrieved January 30, 2021, https://www.pbs.org/wgbh/aia/part3/3p1576.html.

57 Meredith Henne Baker, *The Richmond Theater Fire: Early America's First Great Disaster* (Baton Rouge, LA: LSU Press, 2012).

58 Emy Mays Kelly, *Application for Membership to the National Society of the Colonial Dames of the XVII Century.*

59 "Some Old Surry Families," *The William and Mary Quarterly 16, no. 4* (Williamsburg, VA: Omohundro Institute of Early American History and Culture, 1908), 221-35, doi:10.2307/1922659.

60 John Bennett Boddie, *Virginia Historical Genealogies.*

61 "Nicolson House," Colonial Ghosts, accessed May 9, 2020, https://colonialghosts.com/nicolson-house/.

62 Charles W. Coleman, "The County Committees of 1774-'75 in Virginia: II," *The William and Mary Quarterly 5, no. 4* ((Williamsburg, VA: Omohundro Institute of Early American History and Culture, 1897): 245-55, doi:10.2307/1914928.

63 "Nicolson House," Colonial Ghosts.

64 Gene Goldmintz. *A Guide to the Bellamy Family Papers.* From Special and Area Studies Collections, George A. Smathers Libraries, University of Florida, *The Bellamy/Bailey Family Papers.* https://ufdc.ufl.edu/AA00017204/00005/1x (accessed April 15, 2020).

65 Mary Walker. *Letters to Burton Bellamy, "Pioneer Days in Florida."* From Special and Area Studies Collections, George A. Smathers Libraries, University of Florida, *The Bellamy/Bailey Family Papers.* https://ufdc.ufl.edu/AA00017204/00005/1x (accessed April 15, 2020).

66 Mark F. Boyd, "The First American Road in Florida: Pensacola-St. Augustine Highway, 1824. Part II," *The Florida Historical Society Quarterly, XIV 3* (Florida: Florida Historical Society, 1936), 139–192.

67 George Baumann. *Bellamy Road, Florida, USA - Sign.* July 31, 2013. Photograph. Jefferson County, FL: July 31, 2013. Ancestry. https://www.ancestry.com/mediaui-viewer/collection/1030/tree/16419899/person/18011234582/media/223fda06-3f46-4e4e-a3b3-e0908cf0091b? phsrc=ALT16&usePUBJs=true (accessed April 15, 2020).

68 Sharyn M. E. Thompson, *The Bellamy-Bailey Family Graveyard.*

69 Ruth Blitch, Anna Berkes, and Bryan Craig, "Francis Wayles Eppes," 1995, rev 2007, https://www.monticello.org/site/research-and-collections/francis-wayles-eppes.

70 Ruth Blitch, Anna Berkes, and Bryan Craig, "Francis Wayles Eppes."

71 Ruth Blitch, Anna Berkes, and Bryan Craig, "Francis Wayles Eppes."

72 Ruth Blitch, Anna Berkes, and Bryan Craig, "Francis Wayles Eppes."

73 Mary Walker. *Letters to Burton Bellamy, "Pioneer Days in Florida."*

74 Mary Oakley McRory and Edith Clarke Barrows, *History of Jefferson County, Florida.*

75 Sharyn M. E. Thompson, *The Bellamy-Bailey Family Graveyard.*

76 Mary Walker. *Letters to Burton Bellamy, "Pioneer Days in Florida."*

77 Sharyn M. E. Thompson, *The Bellamy-Bailey Family Graveyard.*

78 Mary Oakley McRory and Edith Clarke Barrows, *History of Jefferson County, Florida.*

79 Mary Oakley McRory and Edith Clarke Barrows, *History of Jefferson County, Florida.*

80 Theodore D. Jervey, "The Butlers of South Carolina," *The South Carolina Historical and Genealogical Magazine 4, no. 4* (Charleston, SC: South Carolina Historical Society, 1903), 296-311.

81 Emma Plunkett Ivy, *As I Find It: a Partially Documented History of Some of the Butlers, Early 1700's to 1968, Including a Few Allied or Related Families. A Partially Documented Record of Some Butler Families of Newberry, Edgefield, Saluda Counties, South Carolina, and of Newton and Rockdale Counties, Georgia* (Atlanta, GA: Peachtree Letter Service, 1968).

82 Pedigree of the Brewster Family, Pedigree Chart #362. Salt Lake City, Utah: Mormon Library.

83 Lucy L. Erwin, *The Ancestry of William Clopton of York County, Virginia: with Records of Some of His Descendants to Which Are Added Royal Lines* (Rutland, VT: The Tuttle Publ. Co., 1939).

84 Emma Plunkett Ivy, *As I Find It.*

85 "Cloud's Creek," accessed April 20, 2020, http://gaz.jrshelby.com/cloudscreek.htm.

86 "James Butler," *Honoring Our Patriots: Pathway of the Patriots.* Washington, DC: DAR. Accessed September 20, 2020. https://honoringourpatriots.dar.org/patriots/james-butler/.

87 Theodore D. Jervey, "The Butlers of South Carolina," *The South Carolina Historical and Genealogical Magazine.*

88 "Women of the American Revolution - Behethland Foote Moore Butler," *AMERICANREVOLUTION.ORG — Your Gateway to the American Revolution.* JDN Group. Accessed June 22, 2020. https://www.americanrevolution.org/women/women40.php.

89 *Revolutionary War Pension, S. 9294, Zachariah Smith Brooks.* South Carolina, 1800 - 1912. From National Archives, *Revolutionary War Pension and Bounty-Land Warrant Application Files, 1775 - 1900.* https://www.fold3.com/image/11987474.

90 John Bailey and Calvert Nicklin, "Descendants of Capt. Robert Behethland of Jamestown." *The William and Mary Quarterly 9, no. 3* ((Williamsburg, VA: Omohundro Institute of Early American History and Culture, 1929): 175-85, doi:10.2307/1921299.

91 Old Simkins Cemetery, Edgefield, Edgefield County, South Carolina, USA.

92 Old Simkins Cemetery, Edgefield.

93 "Oakley Park Plantation, Edgefield, Edgefield County," *Oakley Park Museum.* Edgefield County, SC: South Carolina Historical Society. Accessed August 6, 2020. https://south-carolina-plantations.com/edgefield/oakley-park.html.

94 Jai Williams, "Oakley Park Plantation," *Preservation Of South Carolina.* Plantations and Historic Homes of South Carolina, 2019. https://noloneliness.com/oakley-park-plantation/.

95 Jai Williams, "Oakley Park Plantation," *Preservation Of South Carolina.*

96 "Oakley Park (Red Shirt Shrine & Museum)." Edgefield, South Carolina. Accessed June 30, 2020. https://www.exploreedgefield.com/place/oakley-park-red-shirt-shrine-museum.

97 *The New York Times via The Augusta (Ga.) Herald,* "A NOTABLE SOUTHERN DUEL.; Meeting of Louis T. Wigfall and Preston S. Brooks." November 25, 1897.

98 *The Times-Picayune (New Orleans, Louisiana),* "Fatal Rencontre, pg 2, Thomas Bird, Duel, Edgefield, SC, Brooks, Wigfall, Carrol." November 18, 1840.

99 Mary Oakley McRory and Edith Clarke Barrows, *History of Jefferson County, Florida.*

100 Mary Oakley McRory and Edith Clarke Barrows, *History of Jefferson County, Florida.*

101 "People at the Nacoosa Plantation, Image RC11359." Florida Memory: State Library and Archives of Florida, 1907. https://www.floridamemory.com/items/show/33886.

102 "People at the Nacoosa Plantation, Image RC11359."

103 H. G. Cutler, *History of Florida.*

104 H. G. Cutler, *History of Florida.*

105 "Interview with Parks Carmichael, July 27, 1984" by Sid Johnston.

106 "Interview with Parks Carmichael, July 27, 1984" by Sid Johnston.

BIBLIOGRAPHY

Ackerly, Mary Denham and Parker, Lula Eastman Jeter, *"Our kin";*
the genealogies of some of the early families who made history
in the founding and development of Bedford County, Virginia.
(Lynchburg, VA: J.P. Bell Co., 1930).

"Africans in America/Part 3/Gabriel's Conspiracy" retrieved January
30, 2021, https://www.pbs.org/wgbh/aia/part3/3p1576.
html.

Bailey, John and Nicklin, Calvert, "Descendants of Capt. Robert
Behethland of Jamestown." *The William and Mary Quarterly*
9, no. 3 (Williamsburg, VA: Omohundro Institute of Early
American History and Culture, 1929), doi:10.2307/1921299.

Baker, Meredith Henne, *The Richmond Theater Fire: Early America's*
First Great Disaster (Baton Rouge, LA: LSU Press, 2012).

Baptist, Edward E., *Creating an Old South: Middle Florida's Plantation*
Frontier before the Civil War (United States: The University
of North Carolina Press, 2003).

Baumann, George. *Bellamy Road, Florida, USA - Sign.* July 31, 2013.
Photograph. Jefferson County, FL: July 31, 2013. Ancestry.
https://www.ancestry.com/mediaui-viewer/collection/1030/
tree/16419899/person/18011234582/media/223fda06-3f46-
4e4e-a3b3-e0908cf0091b?_phsrc=ALT16&usePUBJs=true
(accessed April 15, 2020).

Blitch, Ruth, Berkes, Anna, and Craig, Bryan, "Francis Wayles
Eppes," 1995, rev 2007, https://www.monticello.org/site/
research-and-collections/francis-wayles-eppes.

Boddie, John Bennett, *Virginia Historical Genealogies* (United States:
Genealogical Publishing Company, 2009).

Boyd, Mark F., "The First American Road in Florida: Pensacola-St. Augustine Highway, 1824. Part II," *The Florida Historical Society Quarterly, XIV 3* (Florida: Florida Historical Society, 1936).

Broughton, W. Harold, *The Cleggs of Old Chatham: the Ancestry, Family, Descendants of Thomas A. Clegg & Bridget Polk: Their Kin & Events of Interest* (Charlotte, NC: The Association, 1977).

"Cloud's Creek," accessed April 20, 2020, http://gaz.jrshelby.com/cloudscreek.htm.

Coleman, Charles W., "The County Committees of 1774-'75 in Virginia: II," *The William and Mary Quarterly 5, no. 4* (Williamsburg, VA: Omohundro Institute of Early American History and Culture, 1897), doi:10.2307/1914928.

Cutler, H. G., *History of Florida, Past and Present, Historical and Biographical* (Chicago: Lewis Pub. Co., 1923).

Erwin, Lucy L., *The Ancestry of William Clopton of York County, Virginia: with Records of Some of His Descendants to Which Are Added Royal Lines* (Rutland, VT: The Tuttle Publ. Co., 1939).

Foley, Louise Pledge Heath, *Early Virginia Families Along the James River: Henrico County, Goochland County, Virginia* (United States: Genealogical Publishing Company, 1992).

"Gaines' Mill," American Battlefield Trust, April 17, 2020. https://www.battlefields.org/learn/articles/gaines-mill.

Goldmintz, Gene. *A Guide to the Bellamy Family Papers.* From Special and Area Studies Collections, George A. Smathers Libraries, University of Florida, *The Bellamy/Bailey Family Papers.* https://ufdc.ufl.edu/AA00017204/00005/1x (accessed April 15, 2020).

Heard, Phil, *THERE CAME A MAN: The Life and Influence of Richard Johnson Mays On the Development of Baptist Work in Florida.* (Madison, FL: Florida Baptist Historical Society, 2004).

Hill, Dorcas Abney Mays. "[Last will and testament of Dorcas Abney Mays Hill.]" Recorded in Will Book B. Edgefield, SC: Office of W.J. Kincaid, Probate Judge, 1804. (accessed May 2, 2020).

Holladay, Bob. *Tallahassee Democrat,* "FAMU Professor Tells Complex Story of Enslaved Preacher in 'Father James Page' | Holladay." February 5, 2021. https://www.tallahassee.com/story/life/2021/02/05/famu-professor-book-tells-complex-story-enslaved-preacher-james-page-bethel-missionary-baptist/4396546001/ (accessed February 10, 2021).

"Interview with Parks Carmichael, July 27, 1984" by Sid Johnston, *University of Florida College of Law Oral History Collection, Samuel Proctor Oral History Program (SPOHP).* Transcript. https://ufdc.ufl.edu/UF00006321/00001/1x (accessed May 1, 2020).

Ivy, Emma Plunkett, *As I Find It: a Partially Documented History of Some of the Butlers, Early 1700's to 1968, Including a Few Allied or Related Families. A Partially Documented Record of Some Butler Families of Newberry, Edgefield, Saluda Counties, South Carolina, and of Newton and Rockdale Counties, Georgia* (Atlanta, GA: Peachtree Letter Service, 1968).

"James Butler," *Honoring Our Patriots: Pathway of the Patriots.* Washington, DC: DAR. Accessed September 20, 2020. https://honoringourpatriots.dar.org/patriots/james-butler/.

Jervey, Theodore D., "The Butlers of South Carolina," *The South Carolina Historical and Genealogical Magazine 4, no. 4* (Charleston, SC: South Carolina Historical Society, 1903).

Kelly, Emy Mays, *Application for Membership to the National Society of the Colonial Dames of the XVII Century, Dominie Everardus Bogardus.* (Tallahassee, FL: May 25, 1960).

Kleiner, Diana J., *Handbook of Texas Online,* "LYKES BROTHERS," accessed August 5, 2020, https://www.tshaonline.org/handbook/entries/lykes-brothers.

Luginbuel Funeral Home, "Descendants of William Copeland," accessed August 5, 2020, http://assets.luginbuel.com/genealogy/documents/Copeland,%20William%20Family.pdf.

Lykes, Genevieve P., *Gift of Heritage* (Self Published, 1969).

Mays, C. Parkhill Jr., "letter to Mrs. Linda Gramling Demott," (Lakeland, FL: March 16, 2000).

Mays, C. Parkhill Jr., *Proud Heritage: From the Early Settlers of Florida to the Present* (Lincoln, NE: iUniverse, 2007).

Mays, Dannitte H. *The New Enterprise (Madison, FL), Vol. VII - No. 33,* "The Mays' Platform." April 16, 1908. From Library of Congress. https://chroniclingamerica. loc.gov/lccn/sn95047178/1908-04-16/ed-1/seq-1/#date1 =1908&sort=date&rows=20&words=D+H+MAYS&sea rchType=basic&sequence=0&index=0&state=Florida& date2=1918&proxtext=%22d.h.+mays%22&y=0&x=0&-dateFilterType=yearRange&page=2 (accessed August 19, 2020).

Mays, Dannitte H. *The Pensacola Journal, Sunday Morning Edition,* "For Congress, D.H. Mays For Re-election." May 8, 1910. From Library of Congress. https://chroniclingamerica.loc. gov/data/batches/fu_emerson_ver01/data/sn87062268/0 0295865088/1910050801/0320.pdf (accessed August 19, 2020).

Mays, Dannitte H. *The Pensacola Journal, Vol. XI - No. 23,* "Hon. D.H. Mays, of Monticello, a Candidate for Congress." January 26, 1908. From Library of Congress. https:// chroniclingamerica.loc.gov/lccn/sn87062268/1908-01-26/ ed-1/seq-1/#date1=1908&index=5&rows=20&words=Dan nitte+Mays&searchType=basic&sequence=0&state=Florid a&date2=1918&proxtext=dannitte+mays&y=0&x=0&date FilterType=yearRange&page=1 (accessed August 19, 2020).

"MAYS, Dannite Hill (1852-1930)," Biographical Directory of the U.S. Congress - Retro Member details, United States

Congress, accessed August 19, 2020 https://bioguideretro. congress.gov/Home/MemberDetails?memIndex=M000289.

Mays, Mattox. "[Last will and testament of Mattox Mays.]" Recorded in Virginia Deed Book 1 1752-1759. Halifax County, VA: August 16, 1772. (accessed May 2, 2020).

Mays, Samuel E. and Mays, Samuel E., *Genealogy of the Mays Family and Related Families to 1929 Inclusive* (Salem, MA: Higginson Book Company, 2006).

McDuffee, A. L., Historian General, NSDAR, "Lineage Book, Vol. 097" (Washington, DC.: Press of Judd & Detweiler, 1927). Accessed September 21, 2020, https:// www.ancestry.com/imageviewer/collections/61157/ images/46155_b290237-00005?usePUB=true&_ phsrc=OBT1&usePUBJs=true&pId=2693283.

McRory, Mary Oakley and Barrows, Edith Clarke, *History of Jefferson County, Florida* (Monticello, FL: Pub. under the auspices of the Kiwanis Club, 1958).

Milzarski, Eric, "Here Are 6 of the Deadliest Battles Ever Fought," Business Insider, February 25, 2019. https://www.businessinsider.com/ here-are-6-of-the-deadliest-battles-ever-fought-2018-2.

Morris, *The Florida Handbook*, p. 616; E.B. Long, *The Civil War Day by Day*; and Rerick, *Memoirs of Florida*, (New York: Da Capo Press, 1971).

Mutersbaugh, Bert M., *The Journal of African American History, No. 2 ed., Vol. 68: The Background of Gabriel's Insurrection* (Washington, DC: Association for the Study of African American Life and History, 1983), doi:https://doi. org/10.2307/2717723.

Neff, David. *Sign Erected at Site of the Church of Rev. Mease.* Photograph. Hampton, VA: July 10, 2011. Ancestry. https://www.ancestry.com/mediaui-viewer/ collection/1030/tree/16419899/person/19275392224/

media/9e4d7eeb-5572-455e-a7fe-f9be3ae648eb?
phsrc=ALT17&usePUBJs=true (accessed April 15, 2020).

"Nicolson House," Colonial Ghosts, accessed May 9, 2020, https://colonialghosts.com/nicolson-house/.

"Oakley Park (Red Shirt Shrine & Museum)." Edgefield, South Carolina. Accessed June 30, 2020. https://www.exploreedgefield.com/place/oakley-park-red-shirt-shrine-museum.

"Oakley Park Plantation, Edgefield, Edgefield County," *Oakley Park Museum*. Edgefield County, SC: South Carolina Historical Society. Accessed August 6, 2020. https://south-carolina-plantations.com/edgefield/oakley-park.html.

Old Simkins Cemetery, Edgefield, Edgefield County, South Carolina, USA.

Parkhill, John. *Parkhill Diary, Folder 11*. Diary. From The Southern Historical Collection at the Louis Round Wilson Special Collections Library, University of North Carolina, *The John Parkhill Papers, 1813-1891*. https://finding-aids.lib.unc.edu/01826/ (accessed April 15, 2020).

Pedigree of the Brewster Family, Pedigree Chart #362. Salt Lake City, Utah: Mormon Library.

"People at the Nacoosa Plantation, Image RC11359." Florida Memory: State Library and Archives of Florida, 1907. https://www.floridamemory.com/items/show/33886.

Pryor, Nelson A. *Jefferson Journal, Vol. 14 No. 4, sec. Viewpoints and Opinions*, "Passing Parade." August 21, 2020.

Reichel, William Cornelius, *A History of the Rise, Progress, and Present Condition of the Bethlehem Female Seminary, with a Catalogue of Its Pupils, 1785-1858* (Philadelphia: Lippincott, 1858).

Revolutionary War Pension, S. 9294, Zachariah Smith Brooks. South Carolina, 1800 - 1912. From National Archives, *Revolutionary War Pension and Bounty-Land Warrant Application Files, 1775 - 1900*. https://www.fold3.com/image/11987474.

"Richard J. Mays," accessed July 20, 2020, https://floridabaptisthistory. org/richard-j-mays/.

Rivers, Larry Eugene, *Father James Page: An Enslaved Preacher's Climb to Freedom* (United States: Johns Hopkins University Press, 2021).

"Some Old Surry Families," *The William and Mary Quarterly 16, no. 4* (Williamsburg, VA: Omohundro Institute of Early American History and Culture, 1908), doi:10.2307/1922659.

South Carolina Magazine of Ancestral Research, Vol. VII, No. 4 (Fall 1979).

Spencer, L. R., Registrar General, NSDAR, "Lineage Book, Vol. 161" (Washington, DC.: Press of Judd & Detweiler, 1938). Accessed September 25, 2020, https://www.ancestry. com/imageviewer/collections/61157/images/46155_ b290463-00188?pId=3741526.

Tallahassee Democrat, "Parkhill Led Tallahassee Regiment in War." March 28, 1974.

Tallahassee Democrat, "Mrs. D.H. Mays Taken By Death in Monticello." May 21, 1954.

Tampa Tribune, "Widow Of James Lykes Dies In Texas At 85." January 6, 1971.

The New York Times via The Augusta (Ga.) Herald, "A NOTABLE SOUTHERN DUEL.; Meeting of Louis T. Wigfall and Preston S. Brooks." November 25, 1897.

The Times-Picayune (New Orleans, Louisiana), "Fatal Rencontre, pg 2, Thomas Bird, Duel, Edgefield, SC, Brooks, Wigfall, Carrol." November 18, 1840.

Thomas Jefferson to Charles Copland, 10 January 1801. Letter. From National Archives, *Founders Online, Jefferson Papers*. https:// founders.archives.gov/documents/Jefferson/01-32-02-0306 (accessed April 10, 2020). [Original source: Barbara B. Oberg. *The Papers of Thomas Jefferson, vol. 32, 1 June 1800–16 February 1801*. Princeton: Princeton University Press, 2005, p. 421.]

Thompson, Sharyn M. E., *The Bellamy-Bailey Family Graveyard* (Tallahassee, FL: Jefferson County Historical Association, 1985).

Walker, Mary. *Letters to Burton Bellamy, "Pioneer Days in Florida."* From Special and Area Studies Collections, George A. Smathers Libraries, University of Florida, *The Bellamy/Bailey Family Papers.* https://ufdc.ufl.edu/AA00017204/00005/1x (accessed April 15, 2020).

Williams, Jai, "Oakley Park Plantation," *Preservation Of South Carolina.* Plantations and Historic Homes of South Carolina, 2019. https://noloneliness.com/oakley-park-plantation/.

"Women of the American Revolution - Behethland Foote Moore Butler," *AMERICANREVOLUTION.ORG — Your Gateway to the American Revolution.* JDN Group. Accessed June 22, 2020. https://www.americanrevolution.org/women/women40.php.

Wooster, Ralph A. *The Florida Historical Quarterly 36, no. 4, 373-85,* "The Florida Secession Convention." 1958. www.jstor.org/stable/30139845 (accessed June 8, 2020).

Printed in the United States
by Baker & Taylor Publisher Services

Printed in the United States
by Baker & Taylor Publisher Services